NEW CALIFORNIA POETRY

Edited by

ROBERT HASS, CALVIN BEDIENT, BRENDA HILLMAN, AND FORREST GANDER

For, BY CAROL SNOW

Enola Gay, BY MARK LEVINE

Selected Poems, BY FANNY HOWE

Sleeping with the Dictionary, BY HARRYETTE MULLEN

Commons, BY MYUNG MI KIM

The Guns and Flags Project, BY GEOFFREY G. O'BRIEN

Gone, BY FANNY HOWE

Why/Why Not, BY MARTHA RONK

A Carnage in the Lovetrees, BY RICHARD GREENFIELD

The Seventy Prepositions, BY CAROL SNOW

Not Even Then, BY BRIAN BLANCHFIELD

Facts for Visitors, BY SRIKANTH REDDY

Leslie Scalapino

It's go in horizontal

SELECTED POEMS, 1974–2006

UNIVERSITY OF CALIFORNIA PRESS   BERKELEY LOS ANGELES LONDON

NATIONAL
ENDOWMENT
FOR THE ARTS
A great nation
deserves great art.

This project is supported in part by an award
from the National Endowment for the Arts.

University of California Press, one of the most distinguished university presses
in the United States, enriches lives around the world by advancing scholarship in
the humanities, social sciences, and natural sciences. Its activities are supported
by the UC Press Foundation and by philanthropic contributions from individuals
and institutions. For more information, visit www.ucpress.edu.

University of California Press
Berkeley and Los Angeles, California

University of California Press, Ltd.
London, England

Library of Congress Cataloging-in-Publication Data

Scalapino, Leslie.
  It's go in horizontal : selected poems, 1974–2006 / Leslie Scalapino.
    p.   cm. — (New California poetry ; 22)
  ISBN 978-0-520-25461-9 (cloth : acid-free paper)
  ISBN 978-0-520-25462-6 (pbk. : acid-free paper)
  I. Title.   II. Series.

PS3569.C2518   2008
811'.54—dc22   2007050133

Manufactured in Canada

17   16   15   14   13   12   11   10   09   08
10   9   8   7   6   5   4   3   2   1

The paper used in this publication meets the minimum requirements of
ANSI/NISO Z39.48-1992 (R 1997) (*Permanence of Paper*).

*mine goes in and
makes this separation
of them involuntarily
as joy*

to make my mind be actions outside only. which they are. that collapses in grey-red bars. actions are life *per se* only without it.

(so) events are minute — even (voluptuous).

Contents

hmmmm in *The Woman Who Could Read the Minds of Dogs*

Consider certain emotions such as falling asleep,   I said,

(especially when one is standing on one's feet), as being similar
to fear, or anger, or fainting.   *I* do.   I feel sleep
in me is induced by blood forced into veins
of my brain.   I can't focus.   My tongue is numb
and so large it is like the long tongue of a calf or
the tongue of a goat or of a sheep.   What's more, I bleat.
Yes. In private, in bed, at night, with my head
turned sideways on the pillow. No wonder I say that I *love* to sleep.

                                ...

How can I help myself,   as one woman said to me about wanting

to have intercourse with strange men,   from thinking of a man

How can I help myself,   as one woman said to me about wanting
to have intercourse with strange men,   from thinking of a man
(someone whom I don't know) as being like a seal. I mean I see a man
(in a crowd such as a theatre) as having the body of a seal in the way
a man would, say, be in bed with someone, kissing and barking,
which is the way a seal will bark and leap on his partly-fused hind limbs.
Yes. Am I not bound, I guess, (I say to myself) to regard him tenderly,
to concentrate on the man's trunk instead of his face, which in this case,
is so impassive.   Seriously,   I am fascinated by the way a seal moves.

Let me explain what I mean by saying I think about a man
(by simply repeating,   really,   what has been said already
by a man: "What can one *do* with beauty? It's there, it hurts")

Let me explain what I mean by saying I think about a man
(by simply repeating,   really,   what has been said already
by a man: "What can one *do* with beauty? It's there, it hurts")
as being like a baboon.   Whatever we usually say
about the way we think about baboons, i.e.   *per se*   ;
in undressing a man   (such as sometimes when I see him
for the first time,   in public,   on the street   ),
I undress him simply by thinking about the way he walks
as being the way a baboon walks slowly on his hind legs
with his tail held erect with his buttocks   (as a man's
are) bare (a man whom one looks back to see) and hair
on the rest of his body,   and making a sound like a
dog's bark.   So far, the idea of the dog's bark is sim-
ply the way I have found to describe a man's sounds   .

...

Seeing the Scenery

Satisfied this morning because I saw myself
(for the first time) in the mirror as a mountain. I mean by this
I "saw the scenery" in myself. Whereas I had pores
and veins and a brain, I was a mountain in the same way
one has boulders or trees. How would this explain, I wondered,
whatever emotions such as affection, cruelty or indifference I feel?
And I knew no matter how careful one is,
pebbles and grains *will be* modified put in a human form.

...

As Rimbaud said,   I thought today sitting in the library
absentmindedly leafing through a book on the habits of birds,

As Rimbaud said,   I thought today sitting in the library
absentmindedly leafing through a book on the habits of birds,
isn't the way we find happiness precisely by losing our senses
(oversimplified, of course. I was being   facetious.) But still
I can see imitating a bird's call such as that of the fledgling
of a goose or a swan (here I referred to the book) by forcing
myself into a swoon. And,   by way of finishing the thought, I,
for the sake of appearances, since there were people sitting
in the chairs around me, merely sagged forward in my seat and
whistled as if I were asleep. Ssss, it came out, sort of a hiss,
like the noise of a goose. So, almost before I knew it,
I followed this by a low and guttural cough
and leaned forward simply to expel some phlegm. Then quickly
I took a glance around before I wiped my mouth. Feeling weary.
                    ...

[EPILOGUE: *anemone*]

"About the night on which a man said he would spend a 100 dollars
on me",   a woman described,   (and he did use up most of it
simply on taxi fares),   "I was able to describe my feelings:

"About the night on which a man said he would spend a 100 dollars
on me",   a woman described,   (and he did use up most of it
simply on taxi fares),   "I was able to describe my feelings:
by saying it was like being an insect who puts its feelers
out into the flowers of a plant,   and sucks from them,   as we were
(sucking)   from the restaurants and bars of the city
to which the taxi took us. All night we were surrounded by lights.
As I lay back inside the taxi, just waiting for the man to make
arrangements for me   (in regard to *that* part of my feeling,
I would describe the taxi as being more like a buoy),   I had the
feeling (thru-out it) of rising slowly,   and of floating along side
particular spots in the city. By morning,   naturally,   I was sated".

...

"One night,   running after her thru the park",   the man said to me
(and he kept using the word "her", tho he was actually referring to me)

"One night,   running after her thru the park",   the man said to me
(and he kept using the word "her", tho he was actually referring to me)
        ,   "I found,   that the deeper I followed her into the park
(aware, having just left my bed, — after finding that she had left me, —
and gone out looking for her,   that the passers-by had begun to stare,
        since I was calling her name)   ;   far from seeming
to lose contact with my bed in my room,   I was like a water lily",
he said, (smiling at me),   "or a lotus, with a stem attached deep in
the bed of a lake.   Meanwhile, I was running   (altho it seemed like
floating) with my head thrown back, and calling out very loudly LESLIE".

                              ...

we put our heads into the windows of a car which was passing, and,

One woman   (I heard about this several years later)   said   :
"being a prostitute"   (this was said, by-the-way ,
after her telling about approaching with 6 or so other women
2 men in a car,   on a street at 3 am in the city)   ;
"means simply coming out of the hotels and streets of the city
to the car (which is waiting with the men in it) in the same way
that, say,   the feelers of an anemone,   (while being attached
at the base to the anemone)   in order to feed it,   float out
further and further into the water which encircles it. So it was:
we put our heads into the windows of a car which was passing, and,
putting our arms around the necks of the men, began kissing them".

                              ...

(in order, he said, each time he revolved, to spit on the body

He, referring to the incident which occurred when he was a boy
riding a bicycle around and around a block in the city,
(in order, he said, each time he revolved, to spit on the body
of the drunk who was lying on the sidewalk) said: "I felt   not
as if *I* were floating   (since I was hardly pushing the pedals
of the bicycle)   but,   rather, that the surface of the *world*
was whirling. There was the man. Who was curled up in the center.
And he, since he was at the hub of my circuit,   probably saw me,
as I leaned over him over and over to spit on him,   as being
simply like,   say,   the shoots of a plant, e.g.   like shots of
the grass as it flashed over him   (since he was in the center of
the world) i.e. First he would see me. Then the sky. Then me".

                    ...

from side to side — like a fish weaving in and out of the limbs
of plants in the water   (this was the way she moved

Let me explain what I mean by saying I thought about someone
(whom I saw ahead of me on the street one day)   as looking like
    she were wagging her tail in the way someone will sway
from side to side — like a fish weaving in and out of the limbs
of plants in the water   (this was the way she moved
thru the people ahead of me on the street) . Since her arms ,
    (as they were pressed to her sides), looked like the fins
of the fish, and her head was lifted so she could "follow her nose",
she seemed to be swimming ahead as if she had a hook in her mouth .

Instead of an Animal

Seeing as I was willing to give up my seat for the person who said
he had reserved it, first wetting out of my excitement or my worry
or perhaps heat, not only the seat but obviously my own clothes,
it is no wonder that the person was willing to sit wallowing in it;
in that perfumes are made to come from the anal glands of animals.

––––––––

Except for seeing women suckling in public — one time,
two women were suckling at the teats of the nursing mother; the
infant being left to whine while the mother endured these females
feeding off of her. With what concern to her infant when the adult
women had finished with her — otherwise I don't mind.

––––––––

Some adolescents visiting us, having been weaned, wouldn't
guess that adolescents were being allowed
to suckle at their mother's breasts
and expected her to open up her dress in public
letting the as yet unweaned 12 or 15 year old be seen nursing.

Stranger when it is the male opening his shirt in public,
and applying an infant to his chest as if he had breasts.
Not even necessary for the infant to have the nipple.
The children let out a few cries, the man puts them up to let
them suck. Or as easily applies them to his back or his thighs.

———————

Some children of seven to ten years of age or so
were letting each other open their shirts and dresses
and suck on each others' nipples.
No matter that they had flat chests, the rest of the children
clamoring to be put on the older children's breasts   .

———————

In that the infants, as yet too helpless to make the animal
yield to a demand to nurse them,
and, owing to the mothers' anxiety on this matter,
the infants were overseen though they were allowed to eat
at a wet nurse's teat.

Asked why these children of 7 or 8 or so had swollen bellies
so that a child's belly
would resemble the hard belly of a cow or of a mare,
they said
that it was because these children had the habit of swallowing air.

―――――

Instead of an animal, we got an old rag that was rancid-
smelling as if it were an animal.
You know how one can want to roll on it.
You know how one can want to roll on it.
You know how one can want to roll on it.

―――――

Many young females — either unable to find any other outlet,
or   , genuinely interested in the immature males
whom they regard merely as toys —
will do their first fondling and caressing
after carefully undressing some seven or eight year old boys.

Some of the children were aware that the source of this sense
of happiness was in there.
They had only to touch themselves —
pushing their fingers in
there at the opening.

———————

Young females will often compare
their surprise
to the time
when they first became aware
that they were able to suck the fluid out of the male's organ.

———————

Even when the mating couple is seen,
the male is curled like a foetus
his mouth is on the female's breast as if he were eating
while the female is hugging him as if she were holding a rabbit
and feeling its heart beating.

I was surprised that infants produced by these wives
never resembled their mothers;
rather, as soon as they were brought to the mothers' bedsides,
they were seen to have the sweetbread
and the hair that curled as if it were on a ram's head.

———————

Afterall it is the adult male who makes the infantile whining sound
in the five and dime store
while the others are seen outside
one waiting in line
some females make noises to imitate swine.

———————

The adult male who is eating at the dinner table with some people,
for instance, sets his napkin on fire
and lets it blaze as one would light a cat on fire with kerosene
so that
people will imagine a cat flaring up like that under their noses.

This eating and walking at the same time is associated all right

I am not interested in talking to anyone
though it is warm and the wind has come up
as though we were preparing for hurricane weather
I hurry back to my car
and on the way find something anyway in the corner of my pocket.

———————

I ate and there should just be the person who was talking about architects,
or one of the other people I was with
there should be just that person in the world
with no banks or culture.

———————

Went out so I'd take the car and a whole system of banking and money
is
based on a hierarchy
we'd have to have monopolies
for me to communicate with someone who has died.

Starting daylight-saving time tho I will need to read the newspaper
if I am working
on a way of breaking the bank at Monte Carlo
except for knowing someone who has already died
it didn't help me to enter a public building today.

———————

Unemployed though when I heard someone who used an obscene word the
other day
he didn't look as if he were in another world
and so I'm worried
especially in this sultry weather.

———————

I ate and then if I go out anywhere when the weather is sultry as
if it were
the beginning of a monsoon
and I am going to communicate with someone who has died
I will have to have a lot of money.

...

Ate and I'd need to know people who were mercenaries, I'd need to
have the military
if I am going to think of nothing
ex-
cept being in a social hierarchy after I'd died.

———————

I've changed my mind if plants are able to be angry or can have
a
moral being
I'd be part of the social hierarchy
I'd be furiously angry.

...

3. note on the poem:

If these people weren't lying and they don't understand what they
do or say,
is it because I could have been matter or a plant?

If they're not lying and they don't understand what they do or say,
is it because they could have been matter?

I didn't lie,
I never lie
and if they didn't lie and didn't understand what they did or
said,
is it because we could have been matter?

———————

Are these people lying if they went somewhere, are dogs and other
animals lying and wouldn't have any reason for lying?

If these people are jealous — but jealousy is in plants and isn't
related to lying, dogs are jealous

I could have been matter and I feel jealous when I go out in public
when I go anywhere

Considering how exaggerated music is

Crowds are her. It is from them that the
corruptions of a feeling occur in structure.

AFTER LINES BY ROBERT DUNCAN

A man in a restaurant shook hands with someone

describing a story of sexual jealousy, I suppose.

I had a sense of a rush coming from the man being that smug. I wanted to be by myself for the moment since I was drinking coffee. I noticed that people felt snobbery toward a man say coming to a party, sensing his interest in it, and this one man who was there did too. Let's say that I've started to learn the piano because I had decided I would compose some music

he's so angry

———

I'd gone outside that day and so I'd speak to someone using a polite tone. I feel agitated when the weather continues to be warm.

I was in a downtown area that had crowded streets and seemed wealthy and so I worried thinking that I had been overly formal with one person that day. I noticed once at a party that a man thought I was being too polite, but there was a lot of traffic on the street outside. Other people were talking, and I was cordial to him.

During this period I would go out in the afternoons but I'd also make attempts at working.

I'd see any number of people then. A man could want attention from people someplace and be talking about himself and seem polite.

I was barely acquainted with another woman but she was part of a circle of people I used to see at the time. The warm weather continued and I happened to find out that she was not as old as people said she was so I felt very happy. I bought a silk blouse at that point and later became fond of it.

———

I felt that I had a balance unrelated to events or people's attitudes during this period. I had the sense of having lost ground with someone when I met him after not going anywhere for awhile and that something had shifted between me and some other people after a short time.

Their behavior however had not changed and I felt self-confident because I had a sense of things I wanted to do and was planning for the next months.

I'd see people at different places who wouldn't speak to some man because they were parasites.

Someone invited me to lunch on several occasions, though after a few weeks this person began to associate with someone else. I had things I was doing and was very happy during this time, and in the afternoons I'd see the person, whom I thought of as a parasite, going some place with someone and looking very contained.

―――――――

Some people would parrot a certain word or phrase and it remained in fashion. I'd go to parties or went out during the summer evenings and that was the time I felt a sense of pleasure.

I'd go somewhere and the weather was warm so that people in a restaurant seemed to act in an insincere way.

I saw some people in a restaurant who stood out because they were dressed well and I thought of them as being sycophants.

It was easy to embarrass people when he didn't have a job or an income. It is easy to mock an unrelated or individual event if one considers any expression to be sexually connected.

considering how exaggerated music is

―――――

Physical differences in a group made for an incestuous nature among people in a restaurant one time. There is the same feeling in being withdrawn for awhile and then going out frequently.

People came together in an incestuous manner by being somewhat remote from someone and satisfying this impulse. He was reserved when he spoke to people which suggested that he had those feelings.

―――――

I could stay at home and I'd go out. There'd be a group of people in one setting or another who knew each other but gradually I began to feel withdrawn from them anyway.

It was easier to remember what had been said and I'd feel satisfied after going somewhere.

Other people seemed completely internal which I noticed when I'd observed a man for some time and saw that he'd say something about himself and I thought that he should be that entirely and that other people don't go into a sort of public world.

I wanted to be wholly transparent so that I would tell people details of my activities whether I was casual or angry.

I'd go to a restaurant or to the beach and my behavior which seemed to reflect only the surface of what I was thinking was reproduced externally in the jobs other people held.

For awhile I had a job in a store. A person I knew was older than I was and also would be very nervous. He had been feeling jaded and unable to do anything for awhile yet my underlying mood and my emotions were not fixed and I managed to work some during this period.

I'd gone to the post office beginning to walk in that direction when it was already late in the afternoon. I noticed that a woman on the street was not dressed right because she was in her early thirties though I'm not saying that I had any plans for that evening either or had anything I wanted to do until a few days from then.

coming sequence

I was in a downtown area and the sense that I had of someone on the street was that she wasn't spending money, or at any rate hadn't spent any that day.

She still had some money on her and was wearing ordinary clothes so that I had the feeling that I didn't want to talk to anyone then. There wasn't anything I wanted to buy either and I had some money with me. She should be shopping rather than myself and she was walking rather fast so that she was with people ahead of me.

———

The sense I had of a man on the street was that he had a family yet was ambivalent toward the place or setting at that moment, an area where there were small businesses and restaurants, and not where he lives. There shouldn't be any sex say; he should be in a normal state and have no sex actually occur then or around that time and then have it occur later. Have slower ability.

A retarding of his ability in general, not just in this setting; and have other people who were there wearing everyday clothes, walking some.

I saw a man coming out of a grocery store carrying a package of sweet rolls or at any rate something that was sweet. He might live in one of the houses in the area. I'd bought some milk and a few things and I'd just had a feeling of wanting to throw them away, the thought coming to me though I'd just bought them.

I had something I had to do later. I began walking and people were at a bus stop as if they were not going to work but were going out for awhile, for part of the afternoon.

———

This was in a business area and there were shops. People sat waiting at the bus stop in the sun and there was no traffic going by at the time so that I had the sense that they should be satisfied sexually by others and not by me or the others there.

They shouldn't move or should walk around some though their sexual life should occur with someone from outside.

———

I saw some men doing construction work in the street and the feeling I had was that they shouldn't do the work then or walk around. There should be a lack of skill or at any rate no movement occurring so that the surroundings were not pleasant and the area they were in then was affluent, was well-off. Someone who ordinarily was skilled at the time has a lessening or crippling of his ability so that he comes sexually, and people just walking around have this sensation only not strong.

I feel that the people I see are all right — in the sense of not getting very old — as I get out of the area where there are shops, a few houses.

I don't see them walk or move a great deal; and they wear good clothes or everyday clothes.

At the time a man doing construction work in the street comes in that slow delayed way; he is in a sort of public world, working for awhile. Then not working for periods of time possibly.

———————

I got a silk blouse which I saw in the window of a store and later became fond of it and wore it constantly. I hadn't been walking a great deal or moving very much but everything should be delayed, should occur later or should occur slowly.

I went downtown. As someone was walking by he said the word good to himself.

Note on My Writing, 1985

On that they were at the beach — aeolotropic series.

The ship (so it's in the foreground) — with the man who's the beggar in back of it, the soil is in back of him — is active. So it's mechanical — there aren't other people's actions — I don't know how old the man in back is. Who's older than I, desire'd been had by him for something else. I'm not old.

And with him being inactive back then.

––––––

Playing ball — so it's like paradise, not because it's in the past, we're on a field; we are creamed by the girls who get together on the other team. They're nubile, but in age they're thirteen or so — so they're strong.

(No one knows each other, aligning according to race as it happens, the color of the girls, and our being creamed in the foreground — as part of it's being that — the net is behind us).

––––––

I intended this work to be the repetition of historically real events the writing of which punches a hole in reality. (As if to void them, but actively).

Also, to know what an event is. An event isn't anything, it isn't a person.

No events occur. Because these are in the past. They don't exist.

Conversely as there is no commentary external to the events, the children on the playing field can commune with each other. It is entirely from the inside out.

There was when writing the work something else occurring besides what's going on in the segments. But the events do not represent that.

A segment in the poem is the actual act or event itself — occurring long after it occurred; or acts put into it which occurred more recently. They somehow come up as the same sound pattern.

The self is unraveled as an example in investigating particular historical events, which are potentially infinite.

The self is a guinea pig.

The piece in *that they were at the beach* titled "A Sequence" is erotica, a genre being artificial which can 'comment on itself' as a surface because it is without external commentary.

External commentary does not exist as it's being entirely erotica genre, which is what?

By its nature as erotica genre, it is convention. Though it may not have people's character or appear to be social convention. Nor does there appear to be domination.

In a Godard film such as *Hail Mary,* one doesn't know whether it is just its surface or it is from the inside out.

Similarly, in "A Sequence" the surface(s) is (are) the same.

The camera lens of writing is the split between oneself and reality. Which one sees first — view of dying and life — is inside, looking out into untroubled 'experience.'

Which is the beggar who's lying back from the dock (in the above example).

So that repression would not be a way of giving depth.

"Chameleon series" in *that they were at the beach* are (multiple) cartoons, distortions of the (inner) self, which have a slight quality of refined Medieval songs.

Interpreting phenomena is deciphering one's view. This is related to poems which are cartoons or writing which uses the genre of comic books, as commentary being the surface.

The form has the 'objective' quality of life — i.e., the comic book, from which life is excluded, has freedom in the actions of the 'characters.'

.

A recent work of mine in such a chameleon cartoon mode is a short 'novel' titled THE PEARL. It is the form of the comic book as writing. Each line or paragraph is a frame, so that each action occurs in the moment.

The writing does not have actual pictures. It 'functions' as does a comic book — in being read.

And read aloud to someone the picture has to be described or seen and then what the figure in it says read.

So it's private.

Cartoons are a self-revealing surface as the comic strip is continuous, multiple, and within it have simultaneous future and past dimensions.

Being inside each frame, is the present moment. But at the same time the writing (the frame) is really behind, in the rear of 'what is really occurring.' The things are happening out ahead of the writing.

The following is five or more frames:

And there's this pink sky that's in front but as if — beforehand. To the

events (of that night) that entire day goes, and then there's this incredible

vast corrugated rungs of rose colored yet extreme sunset as if it had covered

the sky and is behind it, pushing.

She's driving up the street of small flat porched houses and it's behind

her, and stretching in front as well.

And as if the events are pushed — from it.

What's happened — ? — she'd slept during the day. Checking the man's

apartment, he's not there.

What is in the frame is occurring — but what's going on (which is 'free') is ahead of, being pushed by, the writing.

The title is a reference to the Medieval poem *The Pearl*. But the work is made up, from experience.

There are similar possibilities in using the form of plays composed of poems. These are 'experience' in that the surface is the same: each poem is an act, done by the actor. It takes place exactly in and as that moment.

The actors, as for example in the play *fin de siècle,* can be made to be something other than what they are. Which causes that thing to be gently internalized by them. People don't usually speak in poems. They aren't that. Nobody's any thing.

The setting and tone of these plays are both realistic and artificial.

FROM that they were at the beach — aeolotropic series

Playing ball — so it's like paradise, not because it's in the past, we're on a field; we are creamed by the girls who get together on the other team. They're nubile, but in age they're thirteen or so — so they're strong.

(No one knows each other, aligning according to race as it happens, the color of the girls, and our being creamed in the foreground — as part of it's being that — the net is behind us).

———

A microcosm, but it's of girls — who were far down on the field, in another situation of playing ball — so it was an instance of the main world though they're nubile but are in age thirteen or so.

My being creamed in the foreground — so it's outside of that — by a girl who runs into me, I returned to the gym.

———

It's the past — yet is repressed in terms of the situation itself, poor people who're working, the division is by color. We're not allowed to leave the airport on arriving — others not permitted to stop over — we're immature in age, so it's inverted.

(Therefore receded — we get on the bus going to the city and look around, seeing people dressed shabbily).

A man — I was immature in age — was a stowaway so not having been active, taken from the ship we're on in a row boat.

(A sailor had fallen out of the row boat then, was embarrassed. So it's like paradise — the embarrassment, therefore it's depressed — seen by his waving at us as the other sailors are coming to him).

The class period ending — it's evanescence not because it's in the past, they'd stamped their feet while seated since the teacher hadn't been able to discipline them. She's old — the red hair coloring had been mocked — they're inactive.

(So it's evanescent because they're inactive. Though I am as well. She'd asked me to pull on her hair to indicate it was her real hair, which I do — them being unaware of this — as the class is disbanding, composed of girls and boys).

It is also an instance in the past, so it's depressed — yet the people on the bus aren't nubile, rather are mature.

We're girls — have to urinate which is unrelated to immaturity — refusing to do so in front of others; we require the bus to leave us. Therefore there aren't other people, we urinate, and then look around.

(So it's inactive — is depressed).

Tall, though they are nubile — playing leap frog is out of place; we're required to do so. It's contemporary in time so it's not depressed — I was immature, thirteen in age or so; responding to the other girls kicking as they jumped over some of us.

(So it's not depressed — but not as being active. I'm creamed, until the crowd of girls is pulled off by an instructor who's in the gym).

Attending a funeral — it's contemporary in time, not being in itself depressed; taking a ridiculous aspect — birds that sing loudly in the chapel where the funeral service is being held. The birds are mechanical — so it's being creamed.

(Like in the earlier episode of playing ball. Our being creamed in the foreground of the field by the other girls).

...

He's depressed — by mugging me — corresponds to my having a job

Having an employer, I'd made jokes seen by him to be inappropriate, had offended him — I make jokes because it's in the past (is therefore sentient — I'm fairly immature in age and my offending him is unintentional).

Winos were lying on the sidewalk, it's a warehouse district; I happen to be wearing a silk blouse, so it's jealousy, not that they're jealous of me necessarily.

They're not receded, and are inert — as it happens are bums — so it's being creamed; because it's contemporary in time — jealousy because of that.

―――――――

The bums happen to be lying in the street, it really occurs that I wear a silk blouse.

So it's mechanical — because of the winos being there — not from the blouse which I'd happened to wear though going into the warehouse district.

―――――――

Stevedores — I'm immature in age — who are now made to live away from their families to work, the division is by color; they're allowed to form unions but not act — so it's evanescent.

(Because it's inactive — not just in the situation itself. Or in their later not coming to the docks — so they were striking, regardless of them being fired which occurs then).

The man having been in government — it's evanescent because it's inactive, our being immature in age — he's assassinated at an airport where we happen to come in that morning. We get on a bus which goes to the ocean — it's also beefcake but not because of the man already having died, is mature.

(We haven't seen him — as with the sailors it's contemporary in time).

———————

A microcosm, but it's of sailors — so it's in the foreground, is beefcake — is in the past

(Therefore is contemporary in time while being seen then — so beefcake is in the past — similar to the situation of the other girls also refusing as I had to walk out onto the field, my then being immediately required to — not just in relation to them cooperating then).

...

The reserves — they weren't using the police, so it's inverted — were wearing battle-gear, it's beautiful weather — they were old — is crowded

not occurring now — and their being frightened of the crowd, so it's inverted because of that — I'm there but jealousy on my part, in general — stemming from that

I'm not retroactive — corresponds to making jokes because it's in the past

(Not retroactive because of the beautiful weather. And taking the car to be repaired; the mechanic coming out to test drive, its tires have gone flat in the short time I was in the shop. The man and I get out of the car, laugh, I walk somewhere else to have its tires filled, drive away. Buying a dip stick then, I'd done what was necessary to it myself apparently).

———

Beginning to honk, because a man in a car behind me looked as if he were going to take my parking place, it's near shops, is crowded — I honked before seeing that he's old. And it appearing he hadn't wanted the parking place.

(His being old not mattering because it's crowded — which is transparent, regardless of there being the one parking place — so it isn't sentient)

A sequence

She heard the sounds of a couple having intercourse and then getting up they went into the shower so that she caught a sight of them naked before hearing the water running. The parts of their bodies which had been covered by clothes were those of leopards. During puberty her own organs and skin were not like this though when she first had intercourse with a man he removed his clothes and his organ and flesh were also a leopard's. She already felt pleasure in sexual activity and her body not resembling these adults made her come easily which also occurred when she had intercourse with another man a few months later.

When sexual unions occurred between a brother and sister they weren't savages or primitive. She had that feeling about having intercourse with men whose organs were those of leopards and hers were not. Walking somewhere after one of these episodes she was excited by it though she might not have made this comparison if she'd actually had a brother. At least the woman she had seen in the shower had a leopard's parts. In these episodes when she'd had intercourse with a man he didn't remark about her not being like that. And if women had these characteristics which she didn't it made her come more easily with him.

She overheard another couple together and happened to see them as she had the couple in the shower. The nude part of the woman was like herself and the man had the leopard's parts so that she had the same reaction and came easily with someone, as she had with a sense of other women having a leopard's traits and herself isolated. The man with whom she had intercourse did not say anything that showed he had seen a difference in her and that made her react physically. Yet other women seemed to have a leopard's characteristics except for this one she'd seen.

Again it seemed that a man with whom she had intercourse was her brother and was ardent with her — but this would not have occurred to her had she really had a brother. Yet her feeling about him was also related to her seeing a woman who was pregnant and was the only one to be so. The woman not receiving attention or remarks on the pregnancy excited her; and went together with her sense of herself coming easily and yet not being pregnant until quite awhile after this time.

She also felt that she came easily feeling herself isolated when she was pregnant since she had the sense of other women having leopards' organs. They had previously had children. She was the only one who was pregnant and again she saw a couple together, the man with leopard's parts and the woman not having these characteristics.

Again she could come since her body was different from the adult who had some parts that were leopards', and having the sense of the women having had children earlier than her and their not having younger children now.

————

Her liking the other women to have had children when she was pregnant had to do with having them there and herself isolated — and yet people not saying much about or responding to the pregnancy. She thought of the man coming as when she caught a sight of the couple together — being able to come with someone a different time because she had a sense of a woman she'd seen having had her children earlier. There being a difference of age, even ten years, between a child she'd have and those the other women had had.

She happened to see some men who were undressed, as if they were boys — one of them had the features and organs of a leopard and the others did not. The difference in this case gave her the sense of them being boys, all of them rather than those who didn't have leopards' characteristics and this made her come easily with someone.

It was not a feeling of their being a younger age, since the men were her own age, and she found the men who lacked the leopard features to be as attractive as the one who had those features. She had the feeling of them as adults and her the same age as them, yet had the other feeling as well in order for her to come then.

———

She saw a couple who were entwined together and her feeling about them came from the earlier episode of seeing the men who were nude and having the sense of them being adolescent boys. Really she'd had the sense of the men she'd seen as being adults and herself the same age as them. The couple she watched were also around the same age as herself — the man being aware of someone else's presence after a time and coming. The woman pleased then though she had not come.

She had intercourse with the man who had the features and organ of a leopard and whom she had first seen with the group of men who lacked these characteristics. The other men were attractive as he was. Yet having the sense of the difference between him and the others, she found it pleasant for him to come and for her not to come that time. The same thing occurred on another occasion with him.

———

She compared the man to plants, to the plants having a nervous aspect and being motionless. The man coming when he had the sense of being delayed in leaving — as if being slowed down had made him come and was exciting, and it was during the afternoon with people walking around. He was late and had to go somewhere, and came, with a feeling of delay and retarding — rather than out of nervousness.

men who're
poor and aren't
doing anything

standing in
the sun
by a housing project

their
living in
a motionless way

having been
led later
on

in
the social
world

there not
having been
a
bourgeoisie

had been
prior
to the sense

of
being at war
...

— the earlier life

comes
apart afterwards
      .

The private life of the people
I see
in the vicinity — coming

apart when
it has
an order — though it hadn't
had that

      ...

       — mine

coming apart — when — or because
theirs
does

Boys and men
in the
area where there
are shops
— their life
coming
apart before

the time when
I'd die

— and when
they would
   ...

his — leading
the life
of the donkey

though there'd
been
order in that

way of life
later on

the
motionless way of
life of
the men

by the housing
project

the women
leading
a motionless
way
of life

which is led
later on
in
the social
world

because
of
being motionless

comes apart
then

Boys who'd enlisted
coming back to the high
school to show off in sailor
uniforms

the way
in which
they
were treated
— since
they were   as in
motionless   the sense
                   in my
                   vomiting
                   — occurring
                   once — of
                   not being
                   in
                   life
                   at the time

men having
to
forget coming from

the country — yet
have it
be in ci-
ties — where they
are — to be
bourgeois — feel
confused
and wounded
seeing it

...

Woman wading on long yellow grass.

There's the blue sky. She's wading turmoil and some buzzards are on the grass — that is before her.

Slow low gutting on the long yellow grass.

and the buzzards are on the corpse that is amidst the grass.

hams forward and then back wading — and ahead and behind that in the grass.

In the blue sky. On the slope. hams extended forward. wading.

on it.

rolled down the grass — and the buzzards on one. Cluster flapping.

that is in the blue sky. Cluster flapping on a corpse.

wading on

indentation in the wave of slopes and buzzards start are on a corpse flapping. up.

hams wading up.

in it.

The buzzards in it had been on the corpses, here and there. Flapping cluster in it on one.

the whirr in that the mixing amidst it in the indentation.

pushed into going into the ocean which is at the edge of this. On the rise, with the others, who're churning. The water is heavy, the rise of it. The living have struggled into it. A shot cracks into it. And a corpse boils. The living churning around it. The lighted sea.

The other feels a crack in her side the hip that is soaked hanging in the heavy water.

blood that comes into the sea from the humans.

And wading in who're shooting they keep on going cracks of shots in it.
churning.
heavy mass.
swimming. the rolls. in the waves.

Having the hip that had hung in the water. In the long grass. Weeds entwined dragging the hip leg lying. Slept deeply before. The men on the mounted pickup truck emerges through grass. A shot in the heavy grass. The leg lying twined in the weed and rolling into indentation.

Buzzards fly up.

from a corpse in the indentation flapping on it.

which is turned over on its trunk.

trunk of woman low wading now.

her on the long grass.

Rolling into indentation of reddish cattle with gentle white faces who're kneeling in it. The kneeling gentle cattle beginning to stand frightened.

The leg is soaked. The kneeling cattle standing, settling. the twined grass. in among them.

Slept in a matted indentation with them.

the men out of the mounted pickup truck overseeing muffled.

Lying by the steer it is not double.

There's a puff. Crack of shots muffled.

Morning comes. it does not come, how can it? the thick slurred cattle kneeling eating in the light air.

the lightened white air. Wheeling oneself forward on a cart, a sled — of the leg. On the sidewalk asking money of the passersby — in it — on the sled.

it is free

for the one they think. for that other who's asking for the money.

on the sled — it is.

a soldier affected by the unburied dead covered with the buzzards in the valleys and not turn that inward.

and then he's in the light air

and not figure out how it unfolds

Wheeling on the sled — having slept in the indentation — deer simply have ticks which become huge until they drop off.

a huge tick in the side of having waded.

they began singing — soldiers she meets on the road are a choir and they began singing.

into the area of just pulp — only that

One realizing I have to do this myself.

the leg is soaked. She goes on the sled. There's a sandbar out along stretching on which are corpses the buzzards had encrusting flapping. the light air is coming up. no planet. or orb. an orb floating.

Now it's gone.

And out tangled in the yellow grass, on it. The woman wading. There's a corpse in the grass the buzzards sapping it whirling. It's far gone. in the light air.

it can't be that in the long yellow grass

the hams stretch out and running down the slope in the yellow grass. arms twirling flapping being in the grass.

There are weeds. It's dawn. Encounters sensitive man. as in trunk of seal lying

on her, rearing — their coming. the light air is coming up. entwined thrashing
around. He puts it into her again.

    Him rearing, on the trunk

    He withdraws it, takes it out

    the weeds are still

    He puts it back in — on the trunk

    Him having gotten an erection

    the trunk, the bulb of it in her. after

    the dawn

There was this crescent moon hanging with a bright planet in this blue night sky.
They were low

    in it

    the sack of corpse wavered bulb that was created by some behavior

    they the orbs weren't held

    birds come glancing sucked and then released

    by the one or the people in their behavior

    it's completely irrelevant

                ...

                         the market creating the jewel
                         and be that completely

          what is bothering you
          that you had to be on the street
          I had five children

Why be in the comic book. We simply are in it.

Yet we must try to be in it. I don't know how.

Girl is seen walking on the street black on the bright billowing sky.

She comes up to the (other), and then is on the other side. with the puffed illumined sky before the (other)

reading memory only
is rem

Some homeless people are by the Safeway. where they congregate.

opening tins someone has given them, as she goes out door and by them towards billowing sky.

they're sitting holding the tins

the sky appearing to move

These guys who attack her in the sense of bullying don't do that to the individual. It is to someone. The instigating bully has a way of flattering them — so that they go along with him — in order to have that.

It is not friendship with him

or to them

it's flattery which he reflects back to himself — and seeing this, supposing one sees it — it will not do anything.

they see that

or don't — and it isn't there. They're not interpreting it that way.

Then seeing it on the retina is reading memory only.

They say — who really are all right (if that is) — that to approach anyone or the stream in that manner makes no sense. not that sense is there. it isn't. and we are open.

that we are not to comment on as supposedly we're not objective on these. Whereas, they who are doing the interpreting comment on these — the objective is producing these.

Their producing these — I am and so it meets.

really they do, as I don't see this.

If one even sees it this way — is rebelling

in the desert — dog trotting emaciated on the road.

the dehydrated shrunken remains of cattle which are hung on sticks planted on the roadside as a sign pass on the desert.

Another woman — not myself — says she was riding in a van, she was getting a ride on the desert with some men who'd been in three different wars who were going fishing in Baja.

They were of different ages — are dislocated, start drinking in the early morning

the sun comes on the line

relations are functions — are in brothels. She isn't to say — yet they want feedback to know that she isn't disgusted by them.

Riding in the van on the desert

I was to give a speech — I was to say. it had been advertised, and I was in public before it. the advertising showed a combination they don't like — they didn't speak to me there. I stood in the crowd and they're not speaking.

then I was the only audience — I thought

They left a space around me when I sat down. One of the men about whom I was to speak though he does not like that came up. speaking to me, the only one who would. None of them came to it. People I didn't know came to it.

some other woman — not myself — dreams

I was looking at cut-away model of buildings. Like looking with it being downtown. One of them was my studio. I could see right inside because it was cut away. It was in a wintry place. There was ice all around the building, and the building was burning. So there was this sensation of fire and ice. And everything was going to burn.

There really is no connection between this self and exteriority that is war. and so we are free — exteriority that is going on without us

not in any
of it

we are not.

ridiculing and gang subjection is
exteriority which is not coming from us
and so it meets

The person seated alone their leaving a space around her, is pouring and so are they — they're outside there is no relation to them.
   go forward for there is no relation to them
   hanging pouring for there is no need to

As there is no relation to exteriority — the women emerging in to the Safeway who might have beaten the boy at that age, there was no commentary coming to them

                    there is not coming from
                    them then

The men opening the tins — there is no commentary, who cares

                         from or to them

                    it's invisible to them who interpret
                    this but if one sees that it is that
                    it is not so

and so this has to be serial — with it being in front.

                    desperation is serial
                    and so can't be seen by them

and so it has to be in experience that is in front

        rebelling people on crack is in front
        and so unknown to them

The people who are young or older don't make it — there is not commentary
on it for them
   no one knows anything about it
   In a jazz club the man's playing and everyone's speaking to it chiming in — he
says Pretend to be someone, as if they're not and will not be the next day. Their
faces fall. He's interpreting them back to them.

        might as well be on crack
        don't tell *me*

I realized this he's saying I'm nothing — why do they do that

        and so it is exteriority
        interpreting the inside

and so we're in the comic book because that is just inside
   They can just be the jewel — they don't know it

        as the comic book is invisible to them
        for it is inside, they can be in it

Who are *they*? — their irrelevant

> their saying that we're in narrative as constructed and
> that we should be outside of that — that that is lowly.
> > experience is lower class
> we'll just be mad insane and not be inside. Their saying
> that we are constructed — and they're constructing it.

Trying to reverse us and turn us inside out

...

The child rebelling as completely accepted to it — that that is the mind — is
the comic book

> > weeping is it

> I always thought that my only problem was
> being controlled by them that was true.

> > do without knowing it
> > and so it meets

Nature may have in it an infinity of different kinds of things . . .

In terms of the notion of the qualitative infinity of nature, one is led to the conclusion that every entity, however fundamental it may seem, is dependent for its existence on the maintenance of appropriate conditions in its infinite background and substructure . . . This interconnection can, under appropriate conditions, grow so strong that it brings about qualitative changes in the modes of being of every kind of entity known thus far. This type of interconnection we shall denote by the name of *reciprocal relationship,* to distinguish it from mere interaction . . .

In this process there is no limit to the new kinds of things that can come into being, and no limit to the number of kinds of transformations, both qualitative and quantitative, that can occur . . .

But if *all* things eventually undergo qualitative transformations, then the process described above will never end. Thus we conclude that the notion that all things can become other kinds of things implies that a complete and eternally applicable definition of any given thing is not possible in terms of any finite number of qualities and properties . . .

Thus, we see that because every kind of thing is defined only through an inexhaustible set of qualities each having a certain degree of relative autonomy, such a thing can and indeed must be unique; i.e., not completely identical with any other thing in the universe, however similar the two things may be. Carrying the analysis further, we now note that because all of the infinity of factors determining what any given thing is are always changing with time, *no such a thing can even remain identical with itself as time passes . . .*

. . . we admit also that nevertheless there still exists an absolute, unique, and objective reality.

DAVID BOHM

CAUSALITY & CHANCE IN MODERN PHYSICS

Bum Series

the men — when I'd
been out in the cold weather — were
found lying on the street, having
died — from the weather; though
usually being there when it's warmer

the men
on the street who'd
died — in the weather — who're bums
observing it, that instance
of where they are — not my
seeing that

cranes are on the
skyline — which are accustomed
to lift the containers to or from
the freighters — as the new
wave attire of the man

though not muscular
— but young — with
the new wave dyed blonde
hair — seeming to
wait at the bus stop, but
always outside of the
hair salon

the bums — the men — having
died — from
the weather — though their
doing that, seeing things from their view when
they were alive

so not to
be upper class — the new
wave baggy pants — the
man with the dyed blonde
hair — who's always standing in
front of the hair salon on
the corner

the public
figure — as gentle — as
the freighter and
their relation

that
of the man with the dyed
blonde hair and
new wave attire — and
the freighter

of our present
president — who doesn't
know of the foreign
environs — as vacant — and
to the freighter and
his and its relation

when our present
president is in an inverse
relation to them — when there's
a social struggle in their
whole setting, which is
abroad

the bums — who've
died — but could be only when
they're living — though it
doesn't have desire, so inverse in
that one setting

to their
social struggle in their
whole setting, which is
abroad and its
relation to the freighter

to the person of
new wave attire — that
person's relation to
the freighter

when the bums are not
alive — at this time — though
were here, not abroad — and
not aware in being so of a
social struggle

the man in the new
wave attire — as the relation
of him
being another person — as
the freighter and
his and its relation

the inverse
relation to the freighter
only occurring when that
person is living

the man — who's
accustomed to
working in the garage —
as having
that relation to
their whole setting

I have been — am —
dumb — as the way
in which that would occur — the
bums — not their existence or
dying from the weather — though
the effect of that

for me to
be dumb — to have
been actually stupid — so that
really could occur — the
bums — in an event

so — dumb as an
active relation to
the bums or to the freighter and
the still oil
rigs — on the ocean

to the repair of
the car — so inverse in that
seeing — though
it doesn't have desire — of
the present

as the oil rigs — which
are the freighter — on the ocean — pushed
up to be the relation
with me, by my being — am — dumb — their
to have that occurrence

to have that — for them, some
people who'd had an attitude
of snobbery — always — so that they're dumb — when it's
senseless — that relation with
them

I almost
froze — and realized I
could die from it — when the bums
were in that situation — and then not
caring, though that's not possible

which had been repaired
— to the car — as I
am — when that's
senseless — though
it doesn't have desire — of
the present

the bums —
found later — in the whole setting
— though when the car
hadn't been repaired — and so
their grinding and
movement in relation to it

The Floating Series

Floating Series 1

the
women — not in
the immediate
setting
— putting the
lily pads or
bud of it
in
themselves

a man entering
after
having
come on her — that
and
the memory of putting
in
the lily pad or the
bud of it first,
made her come

having put
the
lily pad in
herself —
encouraging the man
to
come inside
her

a man to
come on the woman
gently — her
having
put the lily pad in
herself
with him not
having entered
her yet

people who're
there
already — though
the other
people aren't
aware of that

not
being able to
see the
other people — and
to be sticking the
lily pad
in
themselves

the man — though
the woman had
come
with
the bud of it
in her
— not having done
so on
that time

or her not
having
put it in — and
the man
coming on her
gently
lying on her
in that
situation

people having
been
there — being
from
the city — already
— and
others not
aware of them

or
having
put in the bud of
it
and
the man not
having
entered her
coming first

that in
the city as in
the middle — to

someone who's
death comes from
age

having
nothing to
do in
a place
— as having
been crazed in
his life-
time

and
having been
aware
before
of others
— who'd
been in
the setting
all along

a man
putting
the lily pad
in her —
after he'd
come — and
she hadn't
on that time

that in
the city as in
the middle — to

someone

the thought
that
they — should be
treated
well — if they'd
paid
their money — or
not

a man's
sense — of — when
he'd come and
she had
the
lily pad in her
and
hadn't come then

the man — on
whom the boy
spit — from him riding his
bicycle by over and
over — was lying on
the sidewalk

not
having
anything to do
as
his having a blockage
with others around
in
the setting

having the
high rents
with
an attitude that
they
shouldn't live in
this
place — who're poor

Floating Series 2

to foresee
the man's
response — when
the woman had
come — him not
having
done so — and
had
the bud of it in her still

the relation
of the public
figure
and
the death at
some time of
the person who dies from
age

                                        and —
                                        — an attitude that
                                        they
                                        should have
                                        a job —
                                        whether they've
                                        means
                                        or not

and —
their — or one's —
having the means
to take care of
oneself or
someone — as
what should
be done

told of
someone being
lower in social
value — that
and in
a setting which defined
us all — when
at that point

their not
to have
a child
— as it happens
— and the bud of
the water lily
in her — when
they'd
been doing it

her having
had
the lily
pad in her still — after
she'd
come — and when there
wasn't
that from it

the crowd
returning when
the man — of their race, though
in the police — he'd
left the van
was immolated by them — on
a field

myself or
a person
aging and dying when
that's seen by
a setting
from — that
of — when
we were young

our
being
that

— as in
the middle

the man — who'd
come
and
with the bud of it
in
her still — when
she had

and — their
sense of the
city — as some
ideal spot
and — where
we're
not going to
be able to live

Third Part

having
swallowed the
water
lily bud — so having
it in
him — when he'd
come on some
time with her

a man'd
swallowed
the bud
of the water lily — and
had
it in
him that way

there
being an
aftermath to   and —
something   a public
occurring   figure — and
                their — not
                based
                in that

                the attitude
                that
                someone — should
                be
                in
                an army — to
                democratize that

— her
coming
when with him — the
lily bud's
being in
the man from
his earlier swallowing
it — him not coming

so that —
with
him
not coming — but
had the
lily's bud in him
as in
other instances

the attitude of
in a setting
aging and dying at
some time
as — that
we
should be
that

— and — a
break through from
a state — of being
crazed — but
which someone
was in

to've gotten
through the
sense — of
being crazed — and
which occurred

and — they
should — be
able
to find some
livelihood — when
they'd been
here awhile

Later Floating Series 1

as
then — what
would be sought after
as valued
by
so many
people — there's
not enough

in
the middle — no
matter — what
the age of
someone — or
if close
to their death — from
age

— and — their
not to be
in it — by virtue
of the
small store — the
setting

Later Floating Series 2

                    someone —
                    as
                    choosing the
                    means —
                    in starting — the
                    small store

— and —
the attitude of
the people frequenting
the shops — as their
a livelihood
for them — the
others

their — wanting
that — the
people frequenting them — for
those
who'd opened the
small stores

his
being
depressed — and to
have
some release from
that — as what
occurs

a break in
— someone's being
depressed — for
him — so
at the time to
have release
from it

in the state that's
his being depressed — and
getting
some charge from inside — that
would get some
release
from that state

— and — the
opening of the
shops — when
many of them
haven't
means — as
for that
situation

Delay Series

*[The series as
qualitative infinity]*

the man — who'd
put out a cigarette after he'd
gotten on the subway — responding
to the cop's bullying who'd seen him
— only — saying he knew of that
rule on it

                                        acknowledging is — when
                                        that
                                        wasn't what was asked — by
                                        the cop on the subway train — for
                                        having had a cigarette on it — to allow
                                        him to fine for that

responding — only
acknowledging one doesn't have that on
the subway — and so
opening up — that as the means of that — without there
being a fight indicated

so the man — as gentle — for
causing the fine — in that situation of
being on the subway — when the cop
had begun to
bully him — at its inception

and — a senseless
relation of the
public figure — to his
dying from age — having that
in the present — as him to us

as is my
relation to the mugger — a
boy — coming up behind
us — grabbing the other woman's
purse — in his running into the park

the boy — who'd
been the mugger — and had run
off into the park — with the other
woman's purse at the time — and that
relation to him

as being the
senseless point — though without
knowing the boy — who was the mugger — after
that — or of course then
either — but that as not being it

it's irrelevant to
want to be like him — whether
it's the mugger — who'd
then run in
to the park — though not that aspect of it

a man — occurring now
dying from being sick — at a young age
— we're not
able to do anything — so fear as an irrelevant
point

the man's death — from
being sick at a young age — as not a
senseless point — not to —
by desire — reach such a thing in
that way

which would be — for him —
fear — whether
it's the mugger — on
our part — but in his
doing that

and — when it could
be reached — though by
him — not by desire on his part — us going in
the cop car after being mugged — when
we'd seen it

where does that
come from — a delay —
not from the mugger — and
on
our part in it

when — that is
that relation —
not the president — which
would then not
be anything

fear — from dying at
a young age — from
sickness — when that emotion is an
irrelevant point — and is
that relation

                                        and — the mugger's
                                        state of mind at the beginning — as
                                        that relation — though
                                        of course afterward he'd run in
                                        to the park

though
— for him — when
that state of mind which is
occurring at the beginning — but
when that aspect of his is of
course an irrelevant point

not in the sense — of
desire — of the mugger's as
that point — on
our part —
occurring at the same time

so — it's an insertion
into
that relation — of someone's
— regardless of
their manner of living

love — on the part — of
the sort of Greta Garbo — so
desire in union with
love — not produced from
it

the man — in a sort of
Greta Garbo — in
a simple union — as being
from desire

and — the man
reversing that — who's
dying at a young age from
sickness — not being that
relation

and — not
it's being the current
relation to
the event — of
it — occurring after that event

and — love finding out
everything — by the sort of
Greta Garbo — the state of mind producing
that — not from him — but as that
relation

                                                  that
                                                  — existing
                                                  in a state of mind
                                                  when that's a
                                                  senseless point

Fin de Siècle 1

A Play

The play is performed by two men. They sit on crates facing out, not towards each other. The poems are spoken by pausing at line breaks and dashes, as if they were songs. They speak simply clearly modestly. Behind them is painted backdrop of expanse of savanna.

I will be — as a construction
1.   — worker
held under — in the world
as a permanent lower class

                          that is — as the
                          construction —
                          worker — not so

that that will be the same — as my own mind — and
it is so — free — with the rest crushing and regarding as
inferior which is nothing there is not that

                                there is not that

    their people — riding on the steppes —
2.   there isn't anything — but
    grass barren vast.

                        we're always asked
                        to take care of
               1.   this other person who is
                        weak and is
                        superior and regarded as
                        that

worker asked to
2. take care of the rest who're strong
and who're seen as that

                  the construction worker is
                  extended so there is nothing
       1.   them — by them — who're
                  strong

                                    who're
                                  weak

goaded so that reaction
is the same — as my
own mind
inside

                  sometimes I wish being a construction
                  worker
                  I were just condemned once and for all
                  to a permanent lower class

a scorching day — walking — and men
on a ladder
2. are up — painting a sign
on a storefront — so work
is inside — them

                  — them
                  inside is movement so
                  walking who's person
       1.   by goes
                  car — by goes cycle
                  weather scorching
                  the — in — painting men

                                many — very — little
                                  words, see

2. free

> that means being
> defined — by them — but
>> 1. if they're not defined by them
>>   which they aren't — they aren't
>>   their class — there is not that

everything is simply doing
as hammering riding
driving

> > > of — the — riding
> > > set
> > > and — don't know
> > > anything
> > > about riding

graffiti on wall do
something with a clear
2. conscience burn a cop
cars going by

> > that — is
> > 1. inside —
> > him

> > > > reach up with
> > > > net, and shown
> > > > by other
> > > > not to catch flying
> > > > jeweled insect

we haven't changed any
from the time of Gengis Khan
we have a fin de siècle
weariness

no, struggle again to
turn insect jeweled
which is flying
not *it*

they're in the corporation
— that are mute
2.
that are out in the breeze
at night

      and if you mutilate
  1. people — they'll
      be beggars

               school says inferior
               construction
           2. worker — for it's
               a corporation, so *not*
               go to it

I'm walking and
this man out says to me
look at that outfit sneering

          misery in
          corporations and then
    1. ɪinefficiency having not
          dunned patients

I'm
getting old, not just to know
one'll die but to be outside

          going by
  (sung   boys who're kneeding
  gently) and molding the dung
          slapped on the walls
          gone from it

                              the hospital foundering on not
                              dunning the patients
                              on time

their in
that

            very heavy
    2.   with child — in the person
            walking out

to turn skater
gladiators — cycle
of the merger
of — successive poor
groups

                        knees up — flesh of on the
                        bicycle
                        crew — though of the one in the
                        flash of them going around the corner
                        in it

they just don't think that
whether the person is mutilated
from stealing matters not
whether there's enough — or
is on the street

                              in
                              around
                              the ring kneeing
                              another — or
                              going by

                                                    legs
                                                    back — around
                                                    the ring
                                                    their
                                                    forward

men crouched or
standing in doorway so they're
floated from their view grainy
there
                        — just in them
                        love — in
              2.
                        their — in the
                        construction
                                        not even
                                        then

the one construction
worker — or man
painting on the storefront — is
just there without the relation to
the others
                                        it had to
                              1.   do
                                        with turning it

they're weak that are out
or the men painting on
    the storefront that
2.
    riding is inside
                        weak
                        is
                        — in them
                        that has
                        nothing

                              they're weak that are in the
                              breeze walking
                              at night the warm weather and
                              ecstatic

                                        developments
                                        waves of them on
                                        hills in them

a ship sailing, pulling
away from dock — its wake
and a man part of the mess crew
in it — working — it on the
mass of water

                              put back through
                              that's
                              not going to seem

small child romping on the hill
like lambs
I.   and newborns and
the adults happy at
the ones

                              man murdered because he's
                              in a section
                              not supposed to be in and is
                              understandable

                                        the construction worker says
                                        the person being murdered
                                        being in that section is understandable

                                                  he says
                                                  this

on bicycle — crew — only there's the
2.   one in it as their flash around
corner

turn that out
— to — the one being outside
who is in
the bicycle crew, which is inside

        flash — of that
        outside
        serene
        which is of
        the one as their there

                to have to care for
                that which he says is
                strong or weak

Fin de Siècle 2

A Play

*The poems are spoken modestly and melodiously by a man (1) and woman (2)
surrounded by a backdrop of a vast savanna. In the distance are scattered hanging
frames (abstract sculptures) of cars.*

went into a camp
1.   in the desert and they were sitting
around a fire out there at night

           no person
       2.   from there
           is present in the ordering
           of the siege
           of their capital

                    war which our country
                    directs and the other foreign
                    capital wanting their capital to fall
                    from their rebels

the newspaper says
what is a newspaper
what are who creating this
being
or are in this

           Chaucer, he knew
       1.   *spring*
           he had spring down

           The army withdrawing — of the Soviets — and into
           the fragile construction — there — conceived
           from a foreign capital — is a siege — which flimsy
           does not collapse their structure

and the prime minister
of the foreign capital
says we are troubled by refugees
but they have a war there

her ministers of the foreign capital
deciding against the siege
2.   and the siege was ordered from there
being
of the other's rebels on their capital

                Not seeing this or remembering as it is real

    people speaking

         when you speak of
      1.   people on the street
         I am that

                  he says and he was
                  in the war

    narration of their construction is
2.
    fragile — being

                    they were hearing my reading and
                    a woman with child — going into
                    labor, it was going to be born

                    the land is thin
                    as — without
                    — the war

   newspaper boy has maroon fingernails
1.   at stand and man makes fun of him
   but he's dying and does, collapsing

                    the maroon fingernails
                    are a symptom which other
                    dying victims have

          virtual doctrine of
          us and the foreign capital
          is that the other capital will fall

                2.   early / from
                      the rebels

      early on in them
1.   or out in they

                            2.   if it does not fall soon
                                  what will become of them

      man in — fragile
1.   capital
      hamburger stands strip

                      it is just merely only beautiful
                      or just only ugly

            just reading

            the newspaper says
        2.   inner chief gains in
              portraying their rebels
              as foreign tools   we are not that
                                           that's not what is meant

      we are thin putting things
 .   on the earth not digging and so
      innocent and hopeful

                            2.   I wrote this and then
                                  I fell asleep

woke up in the morning

        I'm willingly in
        the lowly horde

carts cars going by
clogged
I took a shower in a dream

                I
                got into the shower stand
                stall in a place I'd
                come in

        being thin from the land or
        not putting thing on it and
        technology though as flat
        being
        rather than people in it   so

                                our — not
                                creating it

is
not seeing this or remembering
and so is — that
and is the land

Fin de Siècle 3

A Play

Done in a soft manner by two women who stand separated from each other in a long space, one set a ways back from the other. They use microphones on poles, speaking enunciating slowly with pauses after the poems as from a well or large field. Three of the poems are sung in a melodious soprano and contralto. A few sounds of reed instruments are heard beginning at the second "pause."

1. at night stream-
ing like rats

> crowds of millions tearing at Khomeini's
> corpse for scraps of the shroud
> carrying it trampling screaming trampled
> swaying fealty

> > in the street at night
> > to stop the tanks

> stopped them sometimes
> 2. pulling people out of the trucks
> and rejoiced

> > innocent
> > longing

> 1. soldiers lost in the park

firing of the soldiers who're
from the countryside who do
who'll
shoot them freely

> 2. they do
> firing

man with bird cage up to tanks
says to the soldiers they're animals and
they shoot him in the chest murdering him

soldiers in streets in trucks
down streets
1. who're chanting
down with chaos
down with chaos

                                    the tanks come
                                    through and crush over people
                        2.   and firing lines
                                    some climb into crevices and are
                                    pulled down within range

                    the old men who
            1.   order this wanting
                    fealty from them

                                    octogenarian military men
                                    sitting at a table praising the army
                                    for the massacre after

dictator's military hand in their civil
war ours is supporting is
2.   gunned down
and our official says I am shocked at
the gunning down of
a 73-year-old man

                        I always thought one had to be tough
            1.   I like the lowly
                        because they are tough

            long time when
            there's not saying
            of anything just swimming
            and walking

(pause)

we looked down
from the roof of the capital on
2.   mass of chanting
flocking people up the street
in the moist air

                                  he's depressed that we're who're
                                  who'll
                                  here in the air attacking what is "for
                                  the people"

                                                  we say

                        ————

                      (pause)

you know people through
time and they don't value anyone
1.   and hurt and can't redeem themselves
and don't realize that

                        drunks

                                  the bureaucrats
                          2.   on the roof
                       (sung as if   drinking
                       a Provençal in the sweltering dusk
                       love song)   of the city

            wind wheeling on the pond surface
        1.   while man in rags paces behind park bench
     (sung) back and forth
             back and forth

                              seen under clump of trees
                              hanging over bench
                    (sung)   back and forth
                              back and forth

the proposition:

people here are stopping
2.   people on the street
women stopping men

                    red
                    poppy fields huge
                    heavy drooping swept
                    in the wind

                              row houses and
                              the families're out on their stoops
                              in the heat

                    just go through the city
                    and go into any house
              1.   throws open the door — they don't
                    mind

                         they're fourteen in
                         a room

ducks come down
on the pond surface couples
strolling on the other side in
dispersed formation

                              that is
                    2.
                              random

                              beating sun
                              beating
                              beating

(she runs loping in
a loop several times
slowly forward and then
returning to her place)

                              not quite right
              (she turns
              in a circle)   not quite right

                              not quite right

        just sitting on a bench
        of the dispersed
        benches

                      drank some liquid
                      sitting
                      bowed under the
                      slight shade

the people were out.
the liquid.
some
drank

              then and forward
              runs
              slowly

                              rubbing

shade slight
the under bowed
sitting
liquid some drank

               as no anxiety
               as
               to that

wading in the grass - it is like an elephant
trunk extended
on the trunk

wading on the grass - trunk of woman on the grass
in it

the nudity of poverty
and calm

scratch
on it

dreams of people's abandonment
of each other
where
it is beamed into them

                       or the same

excreting
crowd Jand
not evening or light

the social being
from inside itself

can be approached
calm

(they) like reality
as a function

scratch on it
scratch on it
scratch on it

there's still on the rim of night (having been in it) which is (in night) there as
his horizontal lying rest in snow — breathing in breath 'at' the light day

overwhelming the mark being 'by' his 'action' — there — only. one's — only
breathing in breath — not night or day.

past cold, the man kneeling in snow — outside, one — which is horizontal
waiting — in 'falling snow' overwhelming of the mark, the other being in
it — only. as being the only overwhelming of rim.

that he's — 'running' — by being forward 'lying' which is waiting (outside):
'by' — on the ground in rim of snow dropping on sky and floor only.

him — having an — action — snowing falling itself as the only overwhelming
the rim — flowing on it:

night's dropping — 'there:' as itself overrunning horizontal lying resting itself.
his (this other person's) overrunning is at rim — only — not 'fighting' as: freezing
snowing in it — only.

structure in reverse is the black sky — inside
defining (as, one) — blue destroying — not — gap — where is figures — is
dawn
being the reduction of the sky by (one's) structure not seen after merely but
in being after only.

...

it's enervating to 'unmake' sole connections apparently formed in one's
(cubicles) by having to be in an other ground of them only — as one (only)

the physical body has nothing to do with this

interpretative is the 'fixing', and as such distortion of phenomenal activity (*per se,* not simply fixing the *view* of actions)

an 'outside' outwardly-articulating 'social' interpretation which qualitatively changes the object of its consideration — as does the inner 'warp', which warps in order to see its own reverberation — is there

···

Why would they dismiss it because it's not the same?

It *exists* because it's not the same

···

from the waist — so that, turned the bulb that's oneself (thorax) — only — then — doesn't have any existence — turned (wherever one turns)
as conception — at waist of magnolia buds that exist in the day really
sewing the black silk irises — not when one turned at waist
sewing them, they have no shape literally except being that — from one's hand (being, in the air)
the irises only had existence in the black, before dawn, in fact
a man doesn't want me to become quiet again — go into ocean not weighed of before fighting — ever

formation of that of narrowed to no form in one — of black voluptuous lip — outside — voluptuous lips that (aren't) on black dawn, or before it when it's black.
There was no intention — being done — with their existing.

not weighed before fighting which is the black, weighed, air — not the lips which have no weight — isn't following
if one's not contending . . . so the inner isn't contending either . . . ?

···

there's no time to oneself is the dawn occurring   its rim

it has no rim

pressure so that the mind comes in to the social unit
it isn't done by people, there's no time to oneself (it's done by people
only) — the night, the dawn, there
the constructed unit being no time to oneself — standing being
completely alone
('standing,' as 'walking')

———————

flowering trees float the sky — packed luminous sky of ocean (a sky that is an
ocean)
the group, not having time for oneself, opens that one floated sky

sleep-deprived one
pressure so that the mind comes in to the social unit — only
the flowering trees, that have nothing but swimming on sky

———————

we can not speak as to concentrate on the constructed unit — nor sleep
much and that 'causes' (?) an actual harmony, serial or it's there after a while,
not based on the similarities of the people

the night is exhaustion rains
luminous night while running to the rise

that's dawn is when running to the rise, later
the rise is the floating people

...

their going into houses killing
is the fact —
the fact is delicate — in existence even

...

people love patricians — form is exhausting

one 'has to' exist there. the physical body has no brown night.

...

if the nature of this is struggling wall of birds flying that (aren't) on their
own. if we're not going to do this with people there isn't any existence.

I'm relieved by the wall of birds. one is (in fact) struggling and not with
one's/their existence — it is a fact. this is a light relief.

...

rain through huge red leaves sea — above and below — sea floor

(and) sky — (freezing night) — though leaves sea is at day, rain — man's lying
breathing beside one is enhanced from (and: it being in) night, (night itself: not
from 'freezing night')? — night can 'not' 'be' enhanced 'from' the man's soft
breathing (which is beside one) —

as: rain in it (day, which is the vast red leaves sea)

isn't by the one's horizontal lying breathing. rain lying pouring, sheets — one
is 'by' someone (as not enhancing rain — only)

breathing — running together on the rise. his horizontal lying — 'at' night.

...

physical strength in leaping, hanging, falling which is sometimes on each other — so that hanging they are floating as swaying by each other in the air. reflected as if they were walking on the ground, whereas they're physically beating their own bodies on a wall — that is there the social unit only, as it's in one's frame and flesh.

people sprawled leaning on wall (of subway underground in passing it) — they can't rest

can in subway underground, but not at all, they aren't resting

they have to run as was to the rise, that is their motions.
people sprawled leaning on walls resting are finding or have to find a way to do it.

...

the mind is action literally, not departing from that — being events or movement outside, which is inside, so the mind is collapsing into and as action. — I can't rest, at all now.

this is despair. *for Dante.* if action of events (my mind) were the same as resting, brought to that, in the way the physical body rests outside
one is not having a rim — 'understanding' rather than 'just get rid of one's mind and body — in traveling' — at all —
the physical body, inner, must continue to move only

———————

the day — only — no
— night (which is delicate)
is

walking in the street (once) with someone shopping, for a dinner with others — the sole event of that is, for nothing, pressed up to the thin day ahead of one being (in this present) at the same time —

the events: a rim collapsing (in one) — differing times on the same present — (and one's) — no — bud — one fears that's too fast

the 'two' events are only 'spring' — 'obstructions' — as one won't be in (be) them at the present at the same time — being — no — bud

...

cold — freezing red sky dusk — slice, reduction not existing — walking only as clear — one — outside, dark roses are in it, as freezing red's slice

a half of the night seen, which isn't there yet — sky only is there — at all

bright dark roses — not bud, ever — in the slice only

...

black thorax's hurt breathing weighing that's thin: whereas the minute struggling ahead of hurt one is not split structure there while being it.

the half-cracked black bud that's one 'hurts' — it's joking: struggle as its minute self before — is split structure in one — neck-dawn on the freezing (air, 'a' thin sky — struggling to overwhelm it as: present).

.

gap — *per se* isn't redoing dawn
man dawn in front of whose house recycled bottles are to be picked up by truck — comes out to say to destitute man not to take them — coming before truck

destitute men in freezing rose to collect the bottles with shopping carts
running ahead of the truck — preceding, being preceded — being in the loop
is not reactivity — nothing is merely.

the freezing thin (dawn) as not even blue — as (not) only death (of anyone) —
the blossoming trees aren't — there — burst, as thin without past.

'not' red line-sky or 'one' redoing minute struggle itself — rebelling, there
too.
crashing of bottles of the truck's picking them after in air

suffering isn't too great — because suffering was too great and would be
greater were there authority.

action is only memory. I have to move only.

running behind wallowing ('a' saw). coupled, an action.
running which is in the air before is not weighing. (not at dawn), (yet is).

to reverse occurs even in dreams in the social unit: that's the dream (that it's
not, occurring there) — that its reverse making contact is thoughts an action —
it is —

cello — 'a' saw that was weighing: (not hurt bud) split structure night with
people only.

as it's not in its structure, as it's occurring: 'this is wild' — because weighing
in the air —
with people only? —

(man waiting in past as kneeling in freezing snow — for one — blossoms of
trees (that weren't, yet), at the same time: that are present — (as kneeling in
snow: 'one' as him bursts thin

for Joanne de Phillips, playing Frank Martin's Irish Trio

all — actions in the time in — being one — to give that up?
heavy rain (dawn) — (not dawn itself)
actions can only be in the (inner) foreground — single — brought in. a
muscle wallowing on — weighed — foreground only.

— I could go inward and be completely free without anything.

...

the day — is the mind collapsing on its surface, its own place — ? — by
reading and writing at the same time — by reading only — alone — as solely,
it doesn't come from the woods, not sustaining, the physical body, either.

...

'standing' 'walking' as present — huge crows loaded a tree (past) by me — at
night sleeping — yet the half-cracked black bud (night: only) and thin blue sky,
but as being oneself only, aren't existing either

single thin wall, waves thousands in the freezing sky and empty fields — and
loaded on tree by me — night is half-cracked black bud in one: as, thin blue sky

the two single events at the present (only)

...

the 'pressure' of the 'choked' thick night, in one, single past event, and thin
present sky

the voluptuous choked thick, 'on' night, can't breathe (the hundreds of huge
slightly moving choked: only 'at' night / — 'only' is fear, single crows loading
tree by thin wall) of one, at night — 'their' dawn — as realigning present dawn,
only — ?

one could give up — ?
(as:) 'their' 'dawn' is thin blue of one — ?

...

This is a serial to be in the newspaper. That's all. It has to really be done.

One's mind can't be suppressed. The moon racing in the desert is one resting. The elation is clear and real, that the physical state is endless.

It's printed in installments, so some information is repeated. Sometimes it doesn't introduce anything. Only the fire storm arose from kindling.

Hole of sumo floating on wave is not it. Not wavering sags on the thin surf.

The contrary expectations are seen to be fabricated in the adult, one, who believes the elation is not realistic. One is swimming on the roof with the hose watering it in the inky air.

Soaked pouring crouching at the red ball. The sumo crouched huge on the thin surf a slab has the moon in it.

The moon hangs on the heavy green wave where the sumo's still, vast.

It doesn't create it nor is it in memory.

It's as close as possible to the condition of not actually occurring, while it is here.

Because if it's my mind that's creating it, I can't get to the point where it will not have done that. I can't get it to occur.

Then sometime, cars began to come in cruising, filled with boys leaning out ogling.

The only police came later slowly cruising after the cruising cars packed with boys that went by. The hills were sheets of flames and dissolving frames.

Collapsing locations onto other places scrutinizes them. It doesn't now. Or juxtapose.

It's motionless in one. Objective is only its occurring.

On a bridge, so cars are driving on the jewel of a bay above it.

While Bechtel is reconstructing the oil fields ours have bombed, in the oil fields their foreign workers who're treated like slaves are executed for sympathizing with their invaders.

Their foreign workers can't survive in their own countries. They will then work for Bechtel.

That's a poem.

We work for Bechtel as writers who show the imperial world. So this is for my donor. The subject.

A hundred and seventy thousand infants maybe died there from starving or disease after the bombings.

A crowd here wearing yellow ribbons is crying for infants to be forced to be born.

One separates from them wearing yellow ribbons and running in the dusk.

The woman is in the blue stream floating on the dusk. In pain and jealousy she's able to be touched by someone in the bow. One leans on it bulb from them on the dusk.

Movement (or shape in writing) is a knowledge that isn't one's thinking *per se.* One's thinking by itself is movement that is knowledge.

In a poem I wrote, *way,* I wanted compassion objectively *to be* in the moving shape there, as the form in the series — pressed in its moving of shape in the real events. It occurs not subject to one and outside of one.

I was trying to get a shape, which is in some way a sound, that's movement in location, and is also compassion by itself (objectively) occurring (*not* imposed) in these locations.

The writing is the minute moving or shape of a real event. Sentiment has no relation to existence. It isn't an act?

One is to be divided from one's natural mind as if that were inferior here.

That we are to conform *per se,* is what would not be ugly, be alone.

Where in the minute shape of a sole event one is there — but not in the entire series subject only to its own moving — *where* one is doesn't exist.

Here I resemble the real events *without* a recurring movement as their articulation in language. It's just out there.

Continual worry is barred by the elation in a light lucidity.

A worrying, that is born in external series of events endlessly, always recurring unrelated to one, is the sole inner suppressant.

The clear elation isn't keeping count in endless space, the light at dawn coming up over the city, being in that.

It is worry itself that is death.

This was pleasures for the new person in the city. Only. Small businesses collapsing, shops featuring flimsy items are for survival.

People eating out are close to the sewer class.

Sometime, the long cavalcade of fire trucks came in thousands of them on the empty sailing pillars of the overpass. Sitting on the roof watching them wind slowly in, soaked crouching on it, see the blood red ball floated.

The small shop closes, one after another quickly. Someone or figures sitting in windows of restaurants eating are close.

Their motion is having little, and so occurring.

I only have these thoughts. I can't seem to be someone else, though having the ideal that one should be.

But if one makes only these motions they're making motions there.

There's no relation between reading pornography and justice. The justices see nothing wrong with it for themselves.

His actions make him a distilled cretin. The distilled cretin as the justice bullying women is thereby appointed to the Supreme Court. Actions are reduced to base. Action is that, a base.

That is the point at which madness is produced. Not from oneself.

It isn't produced from dreaming.

Waiting for a dream to come up to observe the day. Not in it. Or compared to it. Nothing's reflected in either then.

One's still fighting inside in it. This produces swimming in one. Then, one dreams.

...

Positions of erotica occur in this which are love then. In those exact minute motions; these have a rhythm of presentation in this that occurs in spurts and not planned. When it is subject to only its movement, it has no other reflection. It isn't social perception; or rather, is it *only* then. What's that?

...

The hyena trotting on the shore slashing at the people as they wade out from the oil on fire comes from (our) fictionalizing. It doesn't have to do with conception. They wade up and are being slashed.

Nature is being socially created yet see it only. It is public solely.

One can drop the pair, but that's where we live. What's that?

Raining, the people standing in it still living, one comes up to them biting to infect them also. Jealous, running at them, who're in the dusk rim being bitten crouch.

My tears are then on a face of a hyena submerged in the air when I'm running. It's on the red ball a retina.

It makes no difference how one responds as long as there is that. The response, there, has to be increased continually, like some still drug. H.D.'s thousand-petalled lily.

Two days after the operation, waking, itself, isn't sustained in a light elation.

One leans over looking into the pool of chest gel the man swimming in it who's serene and gentle. His eyes floating hanging are closed. One needs him for seeing reality. He's hanging in peace but with one not there.

The man puts his long member in one, bending so he's sitting up on her where the sky's vast and red.

He comes with her in the blue dusk rim which is hanging under the sky.

There's a vast breath on the sky like a blister.

Yet wounded the soft breath comes from him. The response is first. The sky's hot, a blue bowl.

This occurrence in it is seeing, which is the only occurrence sustained. One is to be isolated on the blue dusk rim clear.

It's making a picture of something in order to see it, which is different from simply making a picture: it is between being and becoming so that it is already there. That's objects as history.

Coming out of a bush throwing rocks at the businessmen who're beating and kicking a woman in black robes Defoe is fragile as the black robes has stumbled while running and fallen down still holds her infant.
This is part of their reelection campaign maybe.

It's impossible to have one in an occurrence as being entirely separate from articulation is the condition. That's the moon.
I just realized this writing is passive-aggressive, as a form. If it's on ('seeing') something that's real. It keeps disappearing as the occurrence, as the occurrence does.
This is seeing the shape of events of history subject to that arbitrarily seen.

Analyzing the occurrence that can't be seen it splinters in experience infinitely. It recedes continually, causing infinite pain. *It* isn't even there. People are responsible for the invisible occurrences. That's exciting.
I feel elation at evening, not from it, yet look forward to evening by itself. Not producing in one's life.
On it, after the president's son and myriads of others siphoned money from the public, they wanted it to be placid. That's the media. They're toadying jackals. We don't have words.

I keep trying to make these pairs of dissimilarity hold to be peaceful, as a form. To have occurrence as them at the same time.
Government prods the people into cattle chutes where they are robbed by bankers and businessmen. It's easiest to rob the public by working right at the bank.

Where there are only actions they neither concur nor float.
Actions make the blue dusk rim.

Kuwaiti royalty, hundreds of whose guest workers as itinerant labor suffered from their imperial yoke and in the aftermath of the war were executed with no trials or fake ones, has to pay to go to bed with Bechtel.

That's why the war took place. Bechtel beds Kuwaiti royalty.

As their blue sky is fouled by oil, the pinched haunches of our president beds Dead Souls.

Some of our government officials are drawn from the ranks of Bechtel in fact.

Neither can read. They're made to concur. So the form of the serial novel is that.

The writing is to be close as possible to nature itself not actually occurring.

Writing is just mechanical: the condition is clear, as one *is* in sleep when not dreaming.

The sumo low scuttles forward on huge crouching legs and pats the other one. There's no content. The open palms slap and slap from the crouching scuttle on the other sumo's chest. One rushes forward with the weight mounted down on the almost kneeling huge legs so that only the palms move in the blows. His haunches scuttle gently.

This is pushed to where being is narrative solely, contentless.

There is *no* angel running toward one which is the same as resting (not) coming to one in the blazing blue.

They're set in the base of their bodies. Crouched in the setting of this powerful lower setting as base, they come out fighting from it, not where *they* are.

Which could run very fast, from it being weight. The black butterfly in the blue has no weight, and the blue doesn't.

A government can't simply be a business for profit. Then it drops out the people lying on the street who are the inner self.

Schools are not simply businesses but are to cultivate the inner self.

We don't have words at all.

As if sealed in the rose dawn, the first lady runs with the wieners. Her hind legs shaking, she's pulling them out of a woman. That women are to be in the home humbling themselves, who really have to have jobs out of necessity, is uttered by the (former) first lady as her hind parts are shaking when she pulls.

Our (former) vice president tries to turn us against the "cultural elite." Here, the cultural elite are simply people who can read at all.

That's a new poem, as seeing being taken to its first surface.

...

FROM Resting lightning that's night, Friendship

For Lyn Hejinian

...

the land is paired as single — as people
— fish and birds in one's hell

— paper mills — steel factories
destroying — only — rubble — 1.2 billion living

— only — coal thorax night's
brown in the hell — land

...

the land and 1.2 billion living are in
a — one's — thorax — chemical wasteland in

paper mills, steel factories, coal the
waste acid pours as sky into the huge

river — and sky pairs in visible hell of
no seeing and living — workers

in rubble — cubicles — coal thorax floated on barge
wakes

...

hell land brown night's thorax
rubble — living only

there's only living (?) — work is
night — too — wasted mills' — one's — 'not'

— as too —

brown ill   coal   cubicles   'not' one is also
weight
tugs — wake — coal sloughs — only

aren't paired and no sky

———

one's — 'brown.' no night.

gray tenements
— stacks
yet

———

Surrounded by horizontal vast plains of cities, mountains, coal mines, on river —
I dreamt about a man I hadn't seen for ten years — we were going to go to lunch.
I was trying to drive him — to unite him — with my grandmother, who is dead
and who in dreams always turns her face, facing to the side unspeaking. In the
dreams I always know that she is dead.

In this one, I didn't know she was dead, and her face was turned forward to
me. The man's face was turned to the side from me, and then he didn't go to
lunch.

Waking, I feared he'd died. (When I returned home he phoned and said "I had
a dream about you. I dreamed we were going to go to lunch. But then we didn't . . ."

I realized the dream was my mind investigating spatially. It was not that the
man was dead. It was that my grandmother *wasn't,* spatially. They're on the same
horizontal space / time.)

———

gorges — horizontal lightning people

night rain on 'brown' — [stacks waving — there's 'no' night] — one is
in
horizontal lightning people

––––––––

horizontal lightning — making night

'no' 'night' occurs — then. one.

[where there was] 'no' 'night' as there are people. at all there, stacks waving
that's on people however then

(at all there — is horizontal 'there')

––––––––

humps rainless moon —

[not at the same time] no stacks waving — there's 'night'

on humps moon flowing horizontal
high

––––––––

separation of dark humps and
wild moon — when

(with) no horizontal lightning in the
space

neck in it — one's and the high night
is in the humps

people in lines on cliff carrying coal — lines on black humps
black humps of horizontal lightning [not at the same time]

coal — one — 'no' relation of work as people crawling lines on cliff
and — to — black humps moon.
is black humps moon.

---

coal humps — people lines crawling on cliff — on humps
'no' 'night' occurs — then. one.
night's horizontal lightning people [not at the same time] [space]

is

---

people carrying in lines on cliff — people crawling carrying on brown
mounds [not at the same time]

one's — go inward — not night's
yet

---

relation of ('not') dying — to people crawling in lines carrying on mounds
seen — ones
and [not at the same time] river's black humps people as lines crawling carrying
as river

---

not association but space changed
— black humps rainless — only

as prior in brown tenements falls strand river — all no
— social — space ever — thick flowing up flat

[water]

having formed argument as one's being [for one, in infancy
— reciprocating — if not(?)

— 'not' as falls cubicles tenements.

brown falls — small thorax filled — spouts falls
[at the same time then]

———

decks — thick

lines crawling on a mountain to eat at night

———

birds — wakes

cubicles tenements sides pouring factory chemicals from spout — falls — .

brown small thorax fills — not being in oneself — or in them — falls strand
[and] flat water

only living having to die as being that isn't at the same time — one's brown
small thorax — is falls horizontal? there
only

what difference do mountains make? —

'at' night not carrying

one's walking 'brown' night — (walking on water) — people crawling in lines
up
what's the relation to its existing [at the same time]?

———————

'can't face' — (in present is 'at the
same time') the lines of people crawling on coal

carrying — isn't 'facing' the night (?)
land spouts of mills as the same

land — 'not' — on — 1.2 billion — 'facing'
space

one doesn't overwhelm — brown tenements thorax
night's lightning — 'facing'?

———————

peering on dams
crowds

———————

ill ordinary people as entire weight's
sloughs — 'no' 'night'

space — occurs 1.2 billion — land is on them
only

kindness — 's — mountain

a man — the rib cage warm — on his side — night's 'not' — thorax not filled [ever] (whether 'brown' or not, night) — one's

one's

[and] is

———

too — his night — on his side
one — 'by' him (being) — thorax

[beating]. lightning [not at the same time]

———

weight is kindness [and] 'no' night occurring
a man's side — as 'by' — black humps moon
there?

— 'facing' — coal humps river

people crawling lines on coal
are

———

to bring two huge realms — outside one — together — using the tiniest flimsy mode.

·

peering on dams — crowds as we pass through on a ship lightning [not at the same time] no disorder occurs, one's rim
isn't in one — (both large and small is rim)
they —

are (as 'past' pair — as peering on dams) —

---

birds falls horizontal in the period when birds are up — [and] one is.

people not speaking — even — when — [as] birds horizontal (now) — [or are]

[past] falls horizontal (space) is people —

---

she is in 'the realm of death' when she died — but isn't now
— my mind is phenomena — as space in my dream — existing 'only'

— being 'on' water (past) now? — as her not being — is — one — now-existing only

— is myself now, walking on water (past) in brown night there [on water]? — only — at the same time — ?

— 'extreme' is existing only
thinking [my] the man had died was inaccurate — as the dream. It was my grandmother wasn't (dead)

[that being happiness — as the dream being] — one isn't in death except when one died

— ['no'] crowds — spouts pouring
on dams

shores pouring spouts where people are

ships lightning rim

———

ones — rainless humps
black

that are in their crawling lines?
moon

———

dislocation of rim — peering on dams

by one

———

black humps mountains
moon

kindness — 's — man's

lines night

———

"white green" — 'no' — occur in one in dream in a forest
walking — there not to be any — separation between 'that' — being in forest —
there
  only — but the dream is "whitish" rim, 'no eyes' — there — isn't in one
  — is in the dream. — pair only — are 'that'. — "white green" night — is.

the two huge realms — not in one — occur

I feel I'm in a slingshot — a loop

is.

there's
no relation to one's eyes —

just go out.

starry sky — 'to'

people
_____

one on red grass and train
is too

out there

low floating high day indigo 'to'

them red grass train
_____

buttocks into evening walking at — / separate — evening

the flaps of the orchids at evening — not running — thighs

— then — [not at the same time] — 'walk'

fireworks on blackness-field — not train's sound [at the same time]

breathing separated from field

———

'to' indigo

which is people

———

evening

people are — crawling lines night —

———

rest in my arms

[and] indigo 'no' humps lines night 'there'

———

the mind going after oneself
seen for the first time before me
is formed even —

helping one seeing the isolated self

other one isn't in lines crawling

one isn't either being that other
one nor their not being there then

[at the same time]

other one isn't in lines crawling

or *is*

_____

other can't not be there then
[which is 'at the same time']

and one rest in my arms

indigo [and] lines 'there'

crawling on coal night [here] then
other one

_____

humps water
[not at the same time] then
lines night

[*'to' Lyn*]

_____

Saint Colombe — which is — so —
grave and light — at the same time

cello is mounds night

long thighs

operating grass orchids

apart

———

labor orchid lines nights — go out

— [night] — the neck — coal lines —

'walk' 'then' — in evening —

———

coal lines while living

[I feel I'm in a slingshot]

———

'walk' — gap — one —

orchid coal lines evening

space — in them?

———

gray and soft 'no' red indigo
no 'walk' to people

'they' (only they) 'walk' — only — which is
to 'there' — in front — one

'orchids' 'evening' 'walk'

coal evening

crawl thighs

_____

　　their thrown sack — buttocks at night in lightning is only — [as] 'in' dim night

　　buttocks [and] on both ends of one, in night 'at' lightning dim 'only sky' not the same [as] night

　　catching — arms dim night lightened — / illumined

_____

— one
buttocks in ones sack lightning — not dim nights
both.

_____

both.
horizontal beside buttocks on limbs dim night. too.

_____

resting lightning that is night. at all.

beside limbs buttocks both.

where one is just going out.

white night-trees lightning horizontal night beside

one — catching other sack who has leapt — outside of — is beside

in the future — limbs on dim night 'at' one

———

white night-tree is 'at' buttocks — both night

breathing isn't 'at' yet beside white night-tree is windless lightning

———

ones is 'the same' as night-trees — then while

not in lightning — in one

———

port as in night 'or' [which is only] one

people have space in them 'there' or only here, now
crawling lines

night is at the port — 'at' one

———

from fireflies. by people in thunder.

in blackness-rain — breathing separated

walking fireflies

walking fireflies suspended blackness-rain — one

people's suspended whining-hysterics — 'to' — suspending leap 'ones'

walking 'on' fireflies people in blackness-rain

(what difference do 'people' make?)

[fireflies are ahead] walking 'on' — suspending 'them' blackness separated leapt— ones

———

for Taylor Davis

thighs aren't any place for them

[board is with in one.]

mirror which is behind (not reflecting or seeing) board no kneeling or windows fireflies

no kneeling fireflies thighs — ones
[also] 'at' orchids   .

ones-fireflies.

thighs. 'no' neck in night.

people's blackness-rain not being any beside [at the same time]

being beside not being any — people as 'leapt' — and beside — 'one'

green being blackness-rain / none — 'to' one — they are.

skating killing depredations green

fireflies walking green — ones

———————

evening running right toward 'people' not thighs — ones

'in' evening orchids ones legs and feet right toward people

banks river having walked on water 'past' lines orchids

why is running right toward people isn't one — [and] is river — blackness being

toward 'only' and that being orchids flaps [when 'past' people] — when one runs toward

green as night is unmarked

ones run toward — 'people' — 'at' night-greenery there —

Friendship *is a spatial syntax, as if rendering interior that is 'oneself' which is (also) being rendered as space of actual geographical location. It's space-based, written in China while on the Yangtze River and while here.*

Note: 'his' — such as, 'his'-quiet or 'his'-fan — is 'the fact,' is or means 'there is someone else' (aware 'there is someone other').

Separate to the side — continuous — one's

and   a — it's not
refugees — are in   — in —
   — the middle — with   one — outside shape
[famine] — first   — hasn't that space
                                                            ahead in one — [is]

      to walk
in
an unstable and ungoverned country
         array [of] —
armed factions   — to one side
are still — fighting   *outside*
                              [one's breathing]

                              shape, *as shape*, is on the side
                              [as it — at all]

                              one's
                        breathing has to
                                 realign — *to* — it
                        can't — [yet]

the
few trickling — back in
— said [they're]
— dying
of thirst dysentery in panicked

flight

their — refugees
— space — outside — one's
breathing
then
being inside — the *'outside'*

anticipated first, not known before

being heard *when* it hasn't been
heard
first — one

yet — they [factions]
want starving
waiting to feed
ends — them [refugees]

breathing — is
— in — outside — one's
— outside shape
has
forgotten
…

The soft dark sides of the horse lying being kicked in the long grass with their coming through the sea of grass from all sides
to hold too much

The soft dark rolling sides-cage of curled horse lying — mounds in grass They're (their) kicking in at the sides

    train on parch cracks
    is freighter — at night

A man, the interior nature of muscular dove — cage — one stretches out on the throat-breast raking it, the base of it while his dove moves — remaining soaked
one

    not changing
    by
    the middle — being
    in

    one — or side is
    one is that

He applies his brilliant gentle mind to the fact in the grass. The kicking people in long grass yet being a tyrant one is respected *per se.* for that.
    This is not the movement in the grass.
    Nor is their movement zither — we had a zither, as children; there is freighter they are themselves *in fact*
    Hemmed in by the long spears, the other in the middle — spears through grass, the people holding them on the other ends on all sides — the other is hemmed pricking as spear-punctures that are on her sides.
    One first — the other does — runs in before (before them being there) —

One is running out — something occurs *then,* when one is running

not anticipating, as in happiness — running out — before is happy, some-
thing occurring does not change that then. experiencing being happy is in the
present, that it *will* be. (*Is* in the future then, at the same time.)

...

Lear is the viewer. One might even loosen this faculty (sensual as exterior / interior at once) of apprehension further from one's stream. (*Zither* is the rewriting of *King Lear* as Kurasawa's *Ran* — which doesn't have this in it)

A little white owl springs up gliding toward one

the girl with eyebrows curved like bows follows it into the plumed grass
the moon or sun resting on the plumed grass, both then

walk on plumed grass

horse

down crowds coming in from the long plumes eyebrows arch following phosphorescent owl gliding in

in fireflies crowds sides running on its sides

crowds running on its sides wallows on black grass

crowds wallow eyebrows on moon-edged horse-blackness

crowds wallow grass horse gliding moon

eyebrows arching through grass wallow moon

eyebrows wallow crowd on the horse

the man at the café outside in the light appears to be wearing magpie's glistening black feathers gliding blackness
crowd comes in plumed grass to little white owl

head in blackness and running legs in plumed grass

seated roils in sun and moon both then on half-plumed wall-grass
crowd in sun and moon both then wallows on wall-plumes and seated to the side the half

horse
alone walking beside man who's seated at café in glistening black wall to plumed grass in crowd

...

— as freedom in rickshaws
early freedom

ocean ball — in future span sky [is in] — too at all one's —
Two — starting out in rickshaws — no supervision then in the city

early freedom — leading to blossomed spring
separation — as one — leading to bud

— as no authority existing at all is only — so it's not itself even —
children insulted in school racially — too there — early freedom

>nothing is based
>on anything

One exists now on only past (present) as 'nothing' (as that being in fact, events — since placing the past at present *is* dissolved)

Humiliating children regarding their race until they stamped and screamed.

then they did also, the adults got out of the way. the realignment by present-adult didn't work. we're not. past.

to change. the past. 'at' present. *no need.*

She dotes on everything that has balls — to sustain them, fanning their ego, so there cannot be love, that is despair — if one doesn't have balls though one is not sustained

>by anything

Look get this straight, I dote on everything that has balls. [This is said by the Mayfly, who later in the comic book scenario is wearing the swastica.]

Everyone begins writing in in letters, Look, she dotes on everything that has balls, meaning favorably of that.

[Mayfly seated at café table still holds swathed balls and with her glistening sails pinned wide black fans outside: Fact in occurrence (past) — is in one's physical frame — too, dawn.]

Then the ballooned fans turn red in the black sun.

The load is so great one'll have to be carried off to the loony bin and *will* here sustain one —

here we're
pretending

I think we should get to utter level of infant [an inner track of despair] — has something to do with dying one isn't now that's it — but that really — as infantile [thin track, line], humps of the colostomy bags on brownshirts them gliding to one and one hits them swatting with newspaper to have them continue gliding say how.

...

One cannot tell a separation between them with humps gliding and their pretending. One's pretending and theirs are so similar as simply pretending — how are we going to be an infant without being infant?

demystify life — so one can do it.

saw curled woman on motorcycle
another waiting for her — on span ahead

— separated from one's — thorax, there

(not) breathing at all — bursting — breathing there

thorax black in shining blue wide
thin — place — of *their* moving
then one's thorax loosened laughs in space

[One suddenly ceased to breathe seeing a curled woman flying on motorcycle bumble-bee-like on vast bridge span where another woman waited curled on motorcycle ahead at the end of the span. One was asphyxiating. *Then*, seeing them, one laughing and weeping at the same time could breathe. One's response was associated with the recent death of a relative, but the sight (of the motorcyclists) was not related in any way.]

boy on skateboard speeding downhill — the thorax opens — one's

one's — black thorax in pelting rain opens
[separately] *slow*

...

fans-forest. there

yet
'the'.
outer-fan — there is no outer fan — is

his

_____

'reverse grace'
and fans-forest

blackening fan — is wind

one's — as outside walking
[his]

_____

— to
notice
'reverse grace' — him — 'love'
early fan
outer walking

early

      his
— walking on trees
— one — [and] — he — loves — [in the middle]
      his
— walking on trees
'at'
red-rain's fan — early
— and — 'in' night

---

      his
planks as dawn [heart's valve — rungs] — goes on
      opened so people's leaving camps
at night
people's tendons being hacked in many — in
      along —
in planks [his — dawn] leaps one him their — to side
      night
      base — there is no base

breaks past rungs while in their middle —
dawn's
    his — people's — fleeing camps — one's
bursting — 'in' it — separate — is — on his

    his quiet's
[[his] 'heart's' — valve] burst 'on' — a — dawn time — one's

———————

    his quiet's
people fleeing
rungs' planks

    his one's rungs
trees' red-rain's planks

          ...

forest existing
his

a center — hurls —

[just] — [and] one's his-quiet

---

     the airs thin falls
'in' one — to be — close [to it]
     planks — people not caring for one
only — dread — at being
no moving away — in airs early
[captured in life — 'as' dying]
     — as 'shape' of early — one's
— in 'his'-quiet's dawn also —
     no other activities — just one's

thin fans-rose forest existing only
     ...

outer
fan — there isn't any
        — in it

captured in life in utter early
freedom
        and dying / others one
at all

and no outer fan
his

[his — [and]
fans-dawn 'there' — now]

                ...

recent-past events — existing separate
sole
 as present ['in'] — 'is'
crowds crawling on black mounds
 singing — climbing —
one's walking on water 'there'
night — 'his'-base walks thin

 in 'his' present early-'one'

 red trees-fan early-forest

 no time is necessary that's now — is it

 ————

 his base walks
 one's — there's a space — in
between like throwing
— dawn's-trees-fan — is — early-instant's

space — this instant in
 the same
one — one's base walks —
 his-thin
moon's-day early

        he will be outside
this instant's fall fans
        breath's alive at night 'his'
— 'at' night
separately early — where — one's base walks

————————

are — their — rungs — there — breath's — ?
'in'
night — 'at' night
crawling lines on black mounds [coal] and
their climbing at night early — ?

his quiet's — no moving away — captured in life

————————

        a switch

with flowers on it

        to take a switch

with flowers on it — night

additional-
        ly early

— crowds surrounding before — to pull
the place down — they call in the army

    where
one walks on water — his quiet's-
    base — jump [one] in middle 'at'-dawn's
'there'
    'base's' middle 'yet' — [and]
— crowds surrounding —

    — on huge river — one's-dawn's
one jumps to or goes to [it]

    ————

    — not — [captured in life]
[is conflict 'one' — why?]
    — in early
— walking
    one has a pair [is]
at present — 'in' — 'at'
    night's — [it]

['it cannot be known']
falling — at night — in sky sleeping even — as one's
    present
base — space — 'it can be known' — is
    [transgressing social
ridiculed for 'it can be known' — 'in' [there being] 'no child'
    early child thinks
    then, right away — that was
accurate — dawn's at sky
    present
base-falling as fan's present stripping away
    as transgressing 'even'

wide base-falling

...

Astor Piazzola was writing [composing, in his tangos] the struggle of modern life.

EDUARDO SMISSON

The text's internal debate is the author's 'comparison' of her mind phenomena to exterior phenomena, laying these alongside each other 'actually' — such as the mind's comparison to dawn, to magnolias, to color of night, as if these are manifestations of mind phenomena, which they are here.

Placing one's mind-actions beside magnolias (words).

'The same figure repeated everywhere,' a line or passage may recur exactly as slipping out of, returning, slipping out of, a frame of concentration and sound.

pink roses — aren't the pink sun rising — are 'social' *only?* both

"night" on famine — as one — real-time

(walking in garbage it wasn't night) — not in time either

'night' 'night' 'won't ever dis-place it' — it can dis-place it — where it occurs

———

he doesn't trust one because it's one — observation ('so' present-time) of a real-time event (past) — to make these be the same 'in order' to dis-place 'them' and one

———

"famine" "famine" is 'to be' impermanence — not formed event. 'as' quoted event, i.e. seen. — first — early, when one is a child — there

———

"emotion is not the cause of impermanence." *is* it? I've thought it causes. not the cause of events' occurrence (there) *as* impermanence

first seeing the ship or seeing the man dying? — the
ship on the ocean, heavy weighed water — black waves at
dock of "famine" "famine" is emotion adjacent to
observation — unfixed.

or it is the observation / the first real-time event itself
(famine) there? one will not be event.

———

not 'seeing' on 'nature' — or on the mind itself either
— between these? — not between these

neither — yet 'attention' — space? not past.

———

pink roses — aren't the pink sun rising — are 'social'
only? both

"night" on famine — as one — real-time

(walking in garbage it wasn't night) — not in time
either

'night' 'night' 'won't ever dis-place it' — it can dis-
place it — where it occurs

— to make these be the same 'in order' to dis-place
'them' and one

'in order' — in spring, later — both.
as it not being first, but at the same time.

yet to mute one's ego — which is in order for that
ground to *be* there

'in order' — in spring, later — both.
as it not being first, occurrence at all, but at the same
time.

---

weight 'follows' — this 'a' night occurs — 'not the
same thing as' — 'on the same level' — is not following
ever? — 'night' is first to it.

what's place — war in 'night' — which is occurring
now

...

not the day being within the blossom

as in reverse (rather than the *day* in it) — the blossom
isn't in the *day* either

'not a black dawn / a black dawn' is real-time only.

---

wants to see — 'authority' — of 'other' men — from
one, that one would be of only 'them'
there being only 'them' 'so' he is subjunctive

'not a black dawn / a black dawn' is real-time only.

...

is subjunctive — the man starving dying lying in garbage? — there not being black dawn — ?

no. not anyway — that is, anywhere. — or: subjunctive is *only* 'social.' both.

then (when alive). — (subjunctive.) — black dawn isn't? — so it has to pass. both.

———

to ignore one's shape / events 'so' it goes on wildly — *and* — anyway.

magnolia buds — that haven't opened — subjectivity / language *only* — both.

words 'black dawn' as shape (instance that has no 'other' occurrence) which is 'their shape / and their *conceptual* shape.'

to subordinate magnolia buds — that is real-time — both.

———

'not' for there to be 'magnolia bud (not-opened)' —

bud 'dis-placing' is lineage — both. single is 'tree's buds there' (as *only* one's 'social' — at the same time.

a given in space — dis-place blossoming trees.

people's behavior being blossoming trees — *per se* (just as that) — and the action of it (their 'behavior') in the trees blossoming prior — which is separate, sole

bound as 'split' (one's) 'to' conception of change as, or in, behavior —
that was not when a child
rather than in blossoming trees — everywhere as ground
is an ocean here

so 'split' is *that* only — ocean 'in' blossoming trees — 'in fact' has to be to change people's behavior / one's as sole

in fact — itself — isn't *then*. change in blossoming trees occurring prior to (trees). (then blossoming trees being 'social' only.)

———————

the moon is socially-based as emotion is — so it would be itself.

a given in space — dis-place blossoming trees.

...

crushed back the head sees skittering walks — from
hurtling road, greenery
    friends as 'that,' i.e. not existing. are *social. is social.*

    — their back cage's move it, is the light-and-
language? both.
    but the men moving there didn't speak. may.

—————

    if there
    no 'friends' (as *everyone isn't* that) — nothing social —
only being child until dying

    delicate back dies sometime. — but these men's backs
move light here only

...

    moving is floating ears — elephants — a trunk and
face floating on one's ears
    either charging or floating on grass, at once
    man's chest: as trunk floating on ears of elephant's —
he's that, coming. ears on 'trunk recoiled or forward.'

...

hemmed in streaming — being attacked — as
conception *also* —

    others streaming being attacked — all over the place
— she says 'it's never happened to *her*'

    isn't hemmed in streaming walking — there is no
'outside' — ?

    she's so protected — 'it's never happened to *her*' —
and it's everywhere — there's no place. —

------

    as their sense that 'the flesh itself isn't anything' as
opposing others et al

    then it's only one — in their 'social' realm — neither,
as there's no memory et al — and the flesh's 'memory of
being free' 'as' 'there'

    — one's subjectivity / language is their or one's motion
only there?

    seeing being only a motion even (in walking, say)

    one has no back — yet. — not even 'in' 'night' —
not even past movements' 'night' — either — and is
    future 'nights'
    where(?) no movement of one's occurs — future is
same as one's motions without extension *now*

    one's motion ahead — is only one *now* — nights rose

    ...

rode back in on horses raids into their own land —
and were defeated — by modern military that had invaded
grinding them, sent to camps, starved, were executed

he says that mind opposing continually is "insane"
as 'simply' not 'in' fixed or continuing social state — which
there *isn't* — but is conceptualized (and he conceptualizes
it) as shared, *isn't* — either, as the mind *per se* is opposing
fixed state continually

individual motions are dependent — orchids and
one's mind streaming-opposing

––––––––

the fabric of their logic (itself hierarchy) is a 'whole,'
which they say is
'analysis.' — one's 'analysis' of their 'whole' fabric,
they say is a 'whole'
(in order to dismiss it) or they say is "insane" *but it
can't be both* probably
convention of perception — can't be both 'whole' and
'insane' — unless it's theirs (they construct)

they exclude outside

––––––––

the tango is dependent — it disrupts — it goes in and
in to outside

their logic itself hierarchy which they call 'analysis' is
invisible to them —

that is not 'analysis' — because it is 'whole' — merely
excluding 'outside'

must 'accept' death of others. — except them. except him. (can't) is them him *also*.

at *'night' any night* is *can't*

...

motion is forward without one. either sleeping or walking, which are the same.

ears. a recoiled or forward trunk is floating on the ears.

a man's trunk, coming.

a man is the tango. is relentless.

gentleness. it is *speaking — there*. repeats 'just' space.

...

repeats 'just' space

their 'social' realm also extended out there — one's motion without extension in this place forward 'as' *at 'night' any night is can't* and at 'night' 'night rose' — is not the same

one's motion forward — not even there — is at *'night' any night* is *can't* — not the flesh's 'memory of being free' either — 'out there'

...

silver half freezing in day
              elation the
              outside
of the outside sky walking
           rose

silver half freezing in day
              moon's elation
of the outside rose, his seeing
           on both
           'sides'
seeing someone else at all and the
             half freezing
elation of the outside so that's even
            with one
continually over and over one / person
           ...

Standing — wall — wall

rose

and — rose flowers, social — both

conceptually as of dropping (being — or a view) in
space — as dropping 'out' — is not using language, here
either (?) — . slow
(which is 'one walking so slow that outraces eludes them'

to walk so slowly as not to be there with them at all

who 'are social only') — or 'outracing' 'them' ahead. neither
yet one sight at a time — 'retains' — (a sight itself
'retains'? outside)
and sight is only separate from language or
movement —

as dropping out low vertical — night is both, with
no people
but images seen at once, left there, *no seeing either*

is wild moon? in day

a left there — as 'left leg' — the viewer is in a separate
place from what they see (at the moment) always — the
viewer is 'they',
both

running — wall is space —

Living in the subjunctive, social — both — is space —
it's fear propelled — isn't in one (who's in it)
or 'when it's *in* one', may be isn't *in* the others —
existing
there — seeing it in oneself only (as: not coming 'from' them,
but in one 'only' 'then' — is then freely
the relation of suffering et al to space — so it isn't in
black night)

this other sees fear coming 'from' others only — 'there'

so acts as fear in her — which is to become or hurt
them (she's)
is black night subjunctive, no, there

there's only that (one's / their) behavior in relation to
space

...

Oppression is the social space

then
someone else in the social space — 'goes for' 'to' —
perceive what's occurring

the outside isn't fear — *then* it isn't — she 'goes for' the
separation of seeing and being *as* it's occurring, its occurrence
elation
the separation of sight and language *there* — the first
time of the social space

is 'between' 'sky' (sky) — at all — daily — evening
times

...

Separation of space sky rung
                    O
sun there that is outside and outside
                        itself
                        one's
walking rose only and there outside
                        rose O
at side of sky on its vertical space
                        separates

                    …

    comparing the mind to magnolias
or to sky, because one sees.
    but comparing people's actions to sky
or to war to moon outside? is in that space
    then.
    apprehend
    behavior-evening — ferocity even
from just one — where there was no reason
    bewildering — doesn't seem
    'bewildering' if it's huge in multitude.
    indentation so that they're even
one to evening — is no behavior-evening
    any event a random space

                    …

on the 'present' wild friends
are 'there' only, yet not
                        going away
                        either
in the middle is their coming
                        together
as red leaves sea early rim in
                        oneself
or just 'placed' together (to not
                        do that)
then its the disparate as rose
                        outside
                        one

wall standing rose could just
                        'place'
                        together
as evening in the middle of
                        people
                        speaking
and so no space even there
                        one?
freezing pale night at wild (only)
                        day
'there' only, no rose even so can
                        'place'
the day there being no people
                        speaking
                        one

It's go in silver freezing
                    half
                    place
the day there being no people
                    and
seeming as them to be, one silver
                    one
                    (not)
any continuum though is at O
                    also
of sun on space at the sky below
separated from its rose sun

Always stay in
the quiet illumined grass
land — but I can't — do it
there being other people there
                    to
                    just do
it only staying in the grass land
                    illumined
'place' it together is 'land' and
                    comes out
                    just
                    do it

He just stays in
    illumined grass land
                has
    just stayed always in it
                in
    events going on there and
                the
                outside
    of illumined grass land comes
                out

      ...

the turtle is slow
    I've got it
(by singing)
the turtle is slow
    beat beat   the turtle approaching
                              the rose wall?
                             — ow

               add
                                    cello crosses
               itself in
                               space one
                         the later one
in
                         society people
                          when
walking   in
                       city
sloth-terror is on the other side
                       from
                       it
   only — can't leave the side

Where is this   Arcadian land she   says has
been then when we   were there
        taking scathing   cruel   obstructing barrier is
and   "no one felt silenced" — feelings silence? — the
ferocity wasn't   visible apparent
        (to them)
if Arcadia   occurred where *is* it   now?   *when?* if it isn't
now what use is it? changing the past   to praise context
then is phenomena —

                                        comes out
        is seen occurring in the place   some
                        ...

                                                        a
                        barrier of horizontal evening
                        closed vertically so there's no past
                        only it has no side
                                                both
                                        evening
                                        elation
                        ...

        The 'present time' is only *my* previous events
continually — seen (dumb) — then place the present being
in one (and occurring as one) — conceptual 'also', both —
        wall is 'rose'

        events' space to — 'place' in the same 'space'
        only
        not even the present
                        ...

                                    hell
                               -pressure
                                    skin
                     or passages in time
                                      in
           excruciating pain physically so the
                                    time
                                passages
           are gone. lifted, it's go
                               so there's
                                    now
           no time here it is spring bare
                                   limbs
           blossom blossoms 'on' bare limbs
                                  'have'
           the blossoms?

                                    seen
           leaveless forest in dream by
           looking   downwards
           so (?) looking up the next day see
                               leaveless
           fan-forest above
                                   there
           are no 'passages' outside
                                  either
           in time going or one
                              outside rose
           'after one'

                                     ...

Can't be
in   'night'

as outside it is just 'day one's in'

either time or duration

excruciating physical pain hell
                              night *not*

is there.
'night night'

for Petah Coyne, sculptures/walls, a bird
seen in both sides of one wall
                    and
for Philip Whalen at one time

one is in space and
one is in time

                    ...

even   excruciating physical
side   gut tears there on the half closed
                          one
                          blackness reef night
                    to
adore rational one truncated not one
                          in visible
'others' tiers of hierarchy that's at once/
                          both 'experienced'
horizontal spaceless not any in the same
                          place
there with blossoms,   they're
                          both —
          at both 'night' sides

'bowed line' 'boughed line' pouring
stacks
                          horizon stacks

                          re-
                          place
people's single movement with /and
                          one's
other   spring
outside substituted   is their
          words subjunctive night
                          there
                          'not inner'
both.
                    ...

'his' early-walking

                    as

'his' 'base-dropping' there is:
              there is
              'someone else'
        'theirs' there

one's

comprehending 'there to be occurrence
                 on one side' and

there's no 'side' as moon's in space 'his'-
            quiet

        ...

pool of horses   running

on immense gold plain but it is indigo sky
              that's

evening horses running in front of far
               reflecting

water lying on the plain, pool where
           they're
           running
           then

on the floor in evening and lightning
           seen before

           is ahead

FROM 'Can't' is 'Night'

1   re — separation of character and

                              night.

              'no language' 'with it' — movement or language, here

2   the real-time event (occurring) is the only thing there is/ *'was'*
they've destroyed language so we have to destroy it in it not
                        movement

        night exists at day — but is not the same night so

        night is not-existing *then then* is open to the senses

she (someone) says our language is to remove boundless character of

                      night,

that's terror.   when?

their 'lie' — as that one's

      is to substitute for night, hers night 'terror' — say how _____. to

      reverse *'their'* reverse of the boundless character of night can't be

                      said

                  or moved either

even though outside

      blues can't exist outside either — as separation of character and

                      night.

        so it's separation of character and night 2

6   since

an event's — not language — separation of character

                       and

night — is outside movement's — separation of character and

                   night 2

day. as. bud 'dis-placing' is

      lineage. — both. (both the bud and 'dis-placing') single is 'tree's'

                buds

                there

      day. "we dropped a few civilians, but what do you do?" the sniper
      says "1 Iraqi soldier and 25 women and children, I didn't take the
                  shot,

          but 1 Iraqi soldier standing among 2 or 3 civilians,"

          sharp-shooter Sergeant Schrumpf remembering the

          woman going down — "the chick was in the way"

    events are against movement   can't be in

one's movement

'dis-placing' terror by killing. not movement dis-placing language

          the Kurds just move in that space

      waves on a line across it ('we've') courted to fight and

      dropped them to be, were, slaughtered again court

to have them attack on the lands

where they're slaughtered then wave on lines on one side in

space 'we'

label them freedom fighters on the line's other side the same

ones 'we' label terror

ists

as words labels space — one — is there difference between the

'basic space of

phenomena'

phrase

and

the space of planets

moon

outside

movement?

7   "I expected them to surrender I thought they would all capitulate."

in the 3 days that followed,

they did not. — many of the Iraqis, Sergeant Redmond

said, attacked headlong into the cutting fire of tanks

and Bradley fighting vehicles

"I wouldn't call it bravery," he

said. "I'd call it stupidity. we value a
soldier's life so much more than they
do. an AK47 isn't going to do
nothing against a Bradley"
since we're to reverse with 'our' language — boundless

characteristic of night

as   day order

Iraqis are fighting   tanks, aircraft, artillery, prison camps, torture

Sergeant Redmond thinks that's stupid. for him relation

of language to movement: is

none?

the relation of language to movement is: 'none' in order to make

that   relation — *there*

the only chance they have is

at all

night

13   destroy that language

for that

night

there

14   this isn't about suffering we'd be suffering if 'we' *were*

happy

she (someone) says 'our' language is reverse of the bound

less that's terrorist

terror characteristic of night's everything

in my language / is 'ours' only — to enter the boundless

night

night's

without language any

basic space of phenomena's not outside or in — is it *there*

also?

a man (someone) says a (this) syntax is a state of being

insanity — but it's attention only — to itself

I thought attention, and as its subject, cannot be insane? or

may be breaking 'his' reason this   now phenomena

'our' being 'happy' (emotion that's convention) is 'ours'

not

in events outside is insane

the outside and the inside cannot be *there*

in 'our' character? if it is uncompounded

or re — in attention (one cannot be regarding), either —

that

separation of character and

night

night cannot be seen

regarding is separation of one from others   only

here   not-regarding

collective now — having driven the Iraqis insane

attention now is insane — is dependent on the separation

of character and night 2, not in movement — either — them

in 'our' thought, language, 'our' movement is before

(language) and later.

the civilians had to be killed on the road

fleeing Baghdad because they were there as

'we're' (invading)

— is not 'our' movement in that it has occurred already —

the breaking of reason not inside movement of

one's

—   moon and movement — of one's or

at all (and moon) — is the breaking of reason.

one's is 'theirs'

16   it's 'not repeated' — 'to produce' — that is:

            'be-dualistic' — at all

        is   night's space

        even —   not

their — that's outside — despair is one's physical

                            movement bud's

                                    lineage

                                    outside

                                    at once

        on one night

17   to reverse

'our' language's reverse of nights night-boundless-

        ness   or movement

                                    of / in

    one's — disintegrating also —

    skin that's movement only   *then*

                                    'can't'

                                    is

                                    'night'

18   their despair is one's physical movement (not).

                                             language is

                                             crushed.

"2   Iraqis sat in despair." after their dead

                              coincide with night after

          (and after night's over). the breaking of reason — a

                                    man seeing.

19   as if by favoring war

                                        is meant its reverse

                                        reverse trees

                                        (that are)

                                        night characteristic

          I can't see / comprehend it's (before night) 'the basic

                                    space of phenomena'

          phrase

          he's been reversed in language — 'we're' 'killing as its

                                        reverse'

              'our' character is even in night_____say how?

20   the breaking of reason

       is silent seeing   movement (of one's)

       language

since these 're in utter isolation only,   that is

everyone

                    is

as language   as social / *and* dawn.

their despair is one's physical movement (not).

21   long movement (single)   does not repeat

         the outside

'isn't' / 'is' the same as 'his' night crushing language

           of one — night's

              space even?

         he / someone else intends actual

    sky even to reverse its night / as language / one not —

   while (one) dawn-waking actually ('at' dawn *yet* one *there*

             also)

        dawn in the same space

                        as one   is.

someone / it's not possible for him to do any thing even

      without attacking someone else first,   *he can't,*

he's never done so.   defensive

                                    is

be-dualistic

he can't stand (in front of others) without first

                        attacking someone what is

this space   (in front of others)?

        he can't sustain

        others because he

           will not.   *'then'*

                          present.

        isn't reason — reason is insane

                    movement of one's

                    is theirs

                      their despair

      already   it?

      that space / social even and not dualistic isn't

  even

                          because that would be dualistic,

        it   night sky *would.*   'be-dualistic'

                              in   nights not mirror

        and: 'our' tyrant makes / 'is' the war expanding in

        an outside the outside breaking reason

is —

        'isn't' / 'is' — the same as 'his' night crushing language

                                                  of one — night's

space even.   long movement (single)

        sky even to reverse its night / as language / 'one not' —

                        while (one) dawn-waking actually ('at'

                        dawn *yet* one *there* dawn also

FROM The Forest Is in the Euphrates River

...

A

m not either in the family or in the outside why
does she (I) see she is no longer in the

is there   outside by

beside huge numbers peoples surface   cruising

                                                    on

                                                the floor

            of the rose desert is broken floating

                                                one's

        the enflamed iris pushes out on   blossom

                                            ing trees roof
            everywhere   rose

surface   makes a hole in space's

air   from their

            the old as rule the forest is in the Euphrates
                                                    River
Toyota cruisers river falcon enters space of fore

stalling people dying   silent

                        words   first
so, not   from it
plane there whose planes are invisible to birds

colliding with them   where birds

                                           can *see*

the falcon   where is the surface of the rose
                                                 floor everywhere
drones floating killing the insurgents citizens
speaking separate   isn't

(the insurgents' speaking isn't)   first

nor is speaking the event's   *as occurrence*

these   (at) once

is everything only lying   separate
                                            words
                                            one
lies 'night' also   of someone else everyone

                                            (why is)

                                            dawn
        the forest is in the Euphrates River

                                            where
            meeting the dead   occurs

only   asleep, in one
(words) in everyone   harmonious

do 'occur' in present wild friends here
            are their words also   once

in that they're (one's)   as occurrence

events   bound   'night'
only (separate) outside   yet no one is

        one isn't event, except as occurrence

in the outside (either)   can't be   places

one's mind by from first beside any streams of is

                them once one's outside's

        events rose desert is everywhere in
            that peoples cruising their Toyotas on

                        the huge floor

                    break its surface
                black rose day first one

Avril

                                        People cruising

Toyotas the rose desert   breaks

everywhere   because they are on its surface then

                                                    only
a woman ignorant and from eyes blank gloating savaging
others   speaking only   no one speaks there they're

not reflected in her eyes her

                              either for her anywhere

tyranny of inverted in her / gloater's being defined as the
                                              social outside

their kindness   a train hurls on tiers seen in the sky

                              no sight admitted
into the gloating one savaging others then doesn't make

sights   cattle came to a blossom

                                        in others

                              so a man threw a ball

blank to everyone is inverted by her savaging speaking

                                only they cruise the
                                rose train surface

                                                    at
                                                    night

no reflection of anything on the rose floor everywhere

they leave the side

———

Authority or abandoning had to have been before
As in the middle   midst
            so (one) is not outside either first
its / their weight is on (in) horizontal night as day also in

that   place 'trees' 'words'

                    a man regards people as only to serve
                                                            him
sees nothing but matter   anyone   at the
requirement of someone else on the condition of *their*

                                                slav   ery
to him   people given up are not slaves then
                                                            offed
abandoned

                                                            they

are set loose   black smoke comes out of a woman's
mouth   their black flowers there
                            the soldiers walk

authority had to have been (before in one)   so (one)
                                    is not outside either first
the roads to   see
            bombs hidden on the roads, a walking soldier may

be   blown in a road they make

the   invaded the living citizens arrested shot

                              coming to the soldiers
                                      only driving
thin armor chicken-winged holding   it on
the soldiers' arms to their sides

                              at the side of night loose
everywhere
                there is no weight in or on it 'actually'

(it's only)   in occurrence (one's)
so they have 'imagined' 'one' is not there

after or first   no one   outside either
everywhere so   the 'flat' being of plants rose
trees   without their blooming   without

it bloom
she   a man who's kind a man threw a ball leaves

                                        the side

                    ...

As has to
be before crickets seethe sing are being the emerald hills that are

                              a dark blue

                                        day
no cobalt night can be there their singing at once is the emerald

                              hill alongside a dark blue
                                        day only one

's *seeing* its (seeing's) occurring at all is before it's pink clover

                                                  sea

              that authority only abandons and offs would have
to have been that authority's occurrence, (night isn't) the con
                              dition of slavery, *before*

is one
defined from that authority, both, seeing the definition of outside
                                                  and not

                    the people fan out cruising   the rose
                                                  desert

        is not reflected in the pink clover sea on 'a' emerald sound
                                                  hills

              their having hearing is the social and 'night' cruising

                                        the floor
there   see and sea dawn   it's a sea
                    breaks stars them anyone can speak a man

                                                  threw
      a ball

FROM DeLay Rose

Occurrence of one's is without one once

       at once   two people

      in conversation — in outside's motion
                    as Creeley thought
                          words
      and speaking
                    as catching up to being in
                    that motion outside
                          (at) once

                        DeLay corrupts   to
money launder   falling out of

    intimidate lobbies so they're only being   on

one side while government rule is tied to favors on both sides of
floatation for their huge corporations' con   tracting and

officials on the take when they know nothing en events acting

one sun and moon at once by each other day at night *then* and
wrecked Iraq Occur's first   with dome floating our penned
                            starving moved

also then   'our'

      president'd   for photos kiss the green corpses swim

      ing in the flood   than the living   transported in

outside's motion — the occurrence between — as Creeley thought

                                  words

one's to catch up to being (in) one's events   at all? I

'd wake at night having dropped out of being in that event *then*
hav having terror that having to be in one's events and *not* being

in them then *when that* — is that like his in which   occur's *first*

                              where? one is first too / two not
                              caused anywhere they're only once /
                                                        at once
outside of occurrence is_____? not.   Occur's first
                              is therefore also two — he'd
have
sentiments be actions, outside's motion *there* too. To occur first
                              is outside's motion
                                                        of one

In Memory of Robert Creeley

                    ...

DeLay rose and

the flower (rose) yet it's action only outward not vertical or
there   our soldiers do horizontal night raids

          kick the doors down and line up the inhabi

          tants battalions patrol a crowd of young Iraqis

                                                  taunt

          ing them then a rocket-propelled grenade fired

                                        from "insurgents"

sailing into the chest of the driver, Staff Sgt. Dale Panchot it
nearly cut him in half   the death of Panchot changed

                                        them for the

              battalion wrapped the town

          in barbed wire giving the men in it identity cards in

          it's action that isn't split or

English only   if you have one of these, you can come and go, if

you   don't have one of these, you can't

          before taking two men to the river   (can't's)
action isn't outward or horizontal   or

          it was Venus, going away, striking her deconstructed

                                        forehand
with conviction   mazarine elands run

with Venus, not her sister, rising

playing sister Serena in US tennis Open   action's
the gap between sleeping and not dreaming and dreaming and

                                                        waking

both run the plop of the air borne ball from them with Venus's
          or from her   deconstructed forehand (a concept) first

                                        leading them   'our'
president's brother's just now, the middle, detached the poor

from   their

having medical care

        in a law that will lead to detaching them in this eve
rywhere in the country the poor when they're ill or dying will

be uncovered   corpses swim

in   the underwater city   leading

Be uncovered

                                        Containing
          the plomb is being   their / our speaking   (and) *not,*
in *their* hemming her,   ever matching their tones to be one as lo
                              wer there everywhere. so one con
structs *is* listening as this speaking to be   not doing *their*
                              this speaking which is only
their enforcing hemming   one and event   just by being born in
                              this have only this space
in the US, being is (one) out of one's skin yet having thought — is
                              the thought in skin that
          — 'intestine's in one's eyelids'   *is* one's only occurre
                                                              nce
                                                              there
?   moon in space is not in time (with) 'when' one'll in forest
be 'on' speaking, one's to at every instant undo as being, come
                    up to, *as* (in) speaking almost just match and
                              at once sensation
just *not* 'match' their outside (construction) being hemmed there

          '*only* in this space' is same as actions, as 'not' in 'this' time
one's hearing is (in one's actions) doing away with speaking, any
                                                              then

Intestine's in eyelids
no habits one's a plomb of walking and seeing   *that*
                    Yet a person's   'living *to* die'
                                                              is
in and 'is'
forest of people killing and or their seeing that they're
(not) 'people's acceptance' is there at all the same as their being
there
                    also their intestines in their eyelids while
                                                              still living

                                                              One's

a plomb of walking and seeing stopped but as that walking and
                                                              seeing

plomb of corpses that swim at surface underwater
city's   not split between their decomposition and

                                                              night

                                                              either

Addington's having made legal   torture and imprisoning con
structing govt rule   that without detainee's trial or

(there's *no*) charges they're on the mere accusation of their terror

ism   he's (Addington's) chosen as an
architect of their being no law

                    for anyone as their choice lives *to* die

they   *may*

dead to replace schools   do so
                        not split between their decomposition and

                                        night? night
is   one's plomb of walking and seeing and they're

split between what's seen and   people's

'acceptance' as if that were the being (anywhere) but isn't anywh
                                ere a lived plain that isn't there

                                                                        is

plomb of everyone's *there*   *at*/ once for an instant   *all*

outside's the (everyone's) plomb of walking and seeing *also* the

circle   ec   static   and   terror of not seeing?

or even terror of not having that (terror of) as being

dead while *their* 'here'   and (in) Addington's outside motion

is legally the physical tortured peoples there

                                                                        so
cial 'acceptance' is an illusion that is then not there then *either*

the separation between   the
choice of being seeing one's illusion / 'people's acceptance' lived

                                                        and their

'not split between their decomposition and night'   is

                                                        terror

'Really' the dead-loved float away   they don't float   aren't there

                                                        233

                                                                    for one
is 'one's choice to live *to* die'   — in that forest is —

                                                        outside outside?

                                    ...

                A man   leaves   the side

Chaka's   and stars run in day
(Chaka's)   a
whirling dervish there runs at 200 miles an hour where the wind
                                                                    's.

the sensation
                        one's mind undoing and seeing *their* actions and
                                                                one's in

                        that are before, everywhere

events   waking (once) in night   *that*   it's night *also*

                                                        separately there
(is) mine d that's lying-night there was the sense [after? mind *it's*

undoing events to order these — which *there* isn't?   the plomb (or
                        der) that stopping see these (events)

        'is everything only lies?' even is irrelevant as is also some

one's saying *he's* dropped a unity, at all, and *one's* is just to have

a   whereas this is their sentiment also   'whole'   ness
is inaccurate, he says, which is not Grenier's his is wordless *with*
words
                        mine d outside of my seeing my action of *that*
                                                        (ordering),

outside or outside events
before or after mine d] (not) undoing night or in it is   (*'not'* is
a side in we're before these events   )

once stars 'unseen' 'at' and had 'sense' of well-being there

as a child anticipating *there*

being ahead every day in or there wonder of 'what's there?' of

having
these
days ahead   'here' a day's in
the   inclement warm wind blasting fast huge red fall   leaves
the side   seen outside roar

my ine not returning to these waking dur ing the a night and the
sensation not having occurred before myself's a space

stopped night *that* once

there events
unfold outside

...

One wave arises and kills everywhere in the

tsunami floating 'here' on other waves

there are

tears of joy emitted at things 'Is everything only lies?' is

there Chaka flies at two hundred miles an hour in stars

there   though

it's day, both   from cells the bully is in the/her

own

sight of her bullying and hurting others gloats but alter

ed in

her lies, the trapped floating hatred arises in one recepi
ent to wild hatred arises yet one may *(can't)* delay rose

reasonless bully   rose flowers

DeLay (lay/silent flowers) impedes arising   but altered

McClure's word 'reason' is outside clear one sees at once

a *the* moon with Venus   occur's first

star that being

s destroying

anyone
here
theirs are only lies 'people's acceptance' the butterflies

                                                          that

die ever freighter OF METAL is pressed on sky that's
          a   tsunami

                                                       'wave'

                                                    Riding in jeeps
                                                    that run the dunes
peak one

                    on the huge Sahara waves dimpled fold the
instantly crescent   *sun*   though the full moon's also

                                                there hour our

                                                    only here
                r no coincidences that are appearances as one's random e
                vents but (is) here anywhere there's *only* coincidences

at all appre r close so not succession ec   static   that
                    wa
            ndering in the huge sienna red sand black not-construct
                                    ed rock pillars crescent-jagged

        the crescent-jagged black huge buttes-pillars move *on*

        our dilated flat day and night (don't or do/ to have)   *red*
                            sand   , one's in the same place as

outside that's not words work were we're do
                                                while
black stars one's we're   crest
a they
call whoop to each other for the jeeps *to* run the crest of
        as 'yets go!'   one a
        to
dune we come up to each mountain where at once there
                                    ere crescent eclipsed

                                                sun

and any   acts
ours/both: 'both' 'they jet' *from*/and call *ing* whoop and

the jeeps run *to* peak one on the other waves .

Acknowledgments

I would like to thank Fanny Howe for her reading of my text and for her writing and inspiration. I'd also like to thank Mei-mei Berssenbrugge, and other friends who are also publishers of my works, Simone Fattal and Douglas Messerli. I am grateful to my publishers Jack Shoemaker, Steve Clay, James Sherry, Peter Ganick, Lyn Hejinian, Suzanna Tamminen, Gil Ott, and Ed Foster.

Poems in *It's go in horizontal* were selected from:
   Considering how exaggerated music is, North Point Press, 1982
   that they were at the beach — aeolotropic series, North Point Press, 1985
   way, North Point Press, 1988
   How Phenomena Appear to Unfold, Potes & Poets Press, 1991
   Crowd and not evening or light, O Books, 1992
   The Front Matter, Dead Souls, Wesleyan University Press, 1996
   The Return of Painting, The Pearl, and Orion/A Trilogy, reprint by Talisman, 1997
   New Time, Wesleyan University Press, 1999
   The Public World / Syntactically Impermanence, Wesleyan University Press, 1999
   The Tango, text and photographs by Scalapino, collaboration with artist Marina
      Adams, Granary Press, 2001
   It's go in/quiet illumined grass/land, The Post-Apollo Press, 2002
   Zither & Autobiography, Wesleyan University Press, 2003
   Day Ocean State of Stars' Night, Green Integer, Los Angeles, 2007

Other Books by Leslie Scalapino

O and Other Poems, Sand Dollar Press, 1976

The Woman Who Could Read the Minds of Dogs, Sand Dollar Press, 1976

Instead of an Animal, Cloud Marauder Press, 1978

This eating and walking is associated all right, Tombouctou, 1979

The Return of Painting, DIA Foundation, 1990

The Return of Painting, The Pearl, and Orion/A Trilogy, North Point Press, 1991

La Foule et Pas Le Soir ou La Lumiere, French translation, Royaumont, 1992

Objects in the Terrifying Tense/Longing from Taking Place, Roof Books, 1994

Goya's L.A., a play, Potes & Poets Press, 1994

Defoe, Sun & Moon Press, 1995. Reprint by Green Integer, 2002

Green and Black, Selected Writings, Talisman Publishers, 1996

Stone Marmalade (the Dreamed Title), collaboration with Kevin Killian,
    Singing Horse Press, fall 1996

The Weatherman Turns Himself In, Zasterle Press, Spain, 1999

Sight, collaboration with Lyn Hejinian, Edge Books, 1999

R-hu, Atelos Press, 2000

Orchid Jetsam, Tuumba, 2001

Dahlia's Iris — Secret Autobiography and Fiction, FC2, 2003

Designer: Janet Wood
Text: 10.5/13 Adobe Garamond
Display: Adobe Garamond
Compositor: BookMatters, Berkeley
Printer and binder: Friesens Corporation

www.ingramcontent.com/pod-product-compliance
Ingram Content Group UK Ltd.
Pitfield, Milton Keynes, MK11 3LW, UK
UKHW031450010225
454546UK00001B/146